WHAT OTHERS A
BREAKFAST ON THE BEACH

"Burdened by recent events in my family, I took this book with me to the shores of the Andaman Sea off the coast of Thailand. I let the poetic words wash over my hurting heart. It renewed my love for the glory of God's creation. It supplied images for what God is doing in my life through both joy and suffering. I know I will never look at the ocean in just the same way again.

"Even if you don't have an ocean nearby, you will hear the crash of the waves and feel the sand between your toes when you read these pages. Hopefully, like me you will leave the beach with your burdens lighter and your heart filled with gladness at the graciousness and mercy of God."

—**Wanda Stewart,**
Pacific Rim Region
International Mission Board, SBC ,
Bangkok, Thailand

"Mark Jordan's *Breakfast on the Beach* combines solid pastoral compassion with the ancient practice of guided spiritual reflection. The spiritual direction of this book offers a path of growth and personal discernment sorely needed in our Christian journey. At last, vacations can be what our heavenly Father intends for believers. The talents of Mark Jordan's pen combined with the passion of his heart bond together to provide an easy handle on growing in knowledge of ourselves and in deeper love of God. Thanks for this exciting new source of spiritual growth."

—**Dr. Cecil Chambers,** President
Family Matters Consulting, Inc.,
Richmond, Virginia

"Every God-seeker has observed the power of spiritual retreat.   Likewise, it seems that when we are at the beach our spiritual senses are heightened.   In the well written *Breakfast on the Beach*, Mark Jordan shows us why: enjoying the handiwork of God is simply a call to seek the face of God.   This book calls us to make our beach week a time of holy intention; to settle in the sand and let the Spirit of God be just as enthralling as the work of God.   Don't go to the beach without this book!"
—**Dr. Steven Smith,** professor of preaching,
Southwestern Baptist Theological Seminary,
Fort Worth, Texas

"Mark has written a book that will be enjoyable whether you are at the beach or just wishing you were.   It takes simple observations from the beachfront and teaches profound spiritual truths.   It is creative and profound.   I think you will enjoy it as much as I did."
—**Ken Hemphill,**
National Strategist,
Empowering Kingdom Growth, SBC,
Nashville, Tennessee

"If you feel like you need a week away, some quiet time at the beach, then you need to read *Breakfast on the Beach: Finding God at the Water's Edge.* It provides rest for the soul, delight to the heart, and peace in the chaos. Let me encourage you to relax, take some time and have breakfast on the beach with Mark Jordan. It may be the best breakfast that you've ever had."
—**Sammy Tippit,**
International evangelist and author
Sammy Tippit Ministries,
San Antonio, Texas

Breakfast on the Beach

Breakfast on the Beach:

FINDING GOD AT THE WATER'S EDGE

BY

MARK R. JORDAN

Austin, Texas

Breakfast on the Beach:
FINDING GOD AT THE WATER'S EDGE
MARK R. JORDAN

Cover Photograph © 2005 Karen Morgan
All Rights Reserved. Used by permission.
To view Karen's work, visit www.kmorganphoto.com
Cover Design and Graphics: Michael Qualben
Pen and Ink Illustrations by the Author

Unless otherwise noted, Scripture quotations are from the *New American Standard Bible,* © The Lockman Foundation (1960,1962,1963, 1968,1971,1972,1973,1975,1977,1995). Used by permission. Other versions cited are: **Amplified,** *The Amplified® Bible,* Grand Rapids: Zondervan (1965); **ESV,** *The Holy Bible,* English Standard Version, Wheaton: Crossway Books (2001); **HCSB,** *Holman Christian Standard Bible,* Nashville: Holman Bible Publishers (2000); **KJV,** *King James Version of the Bible;* **The Message,** *The Message,* Colorado Springs: Navpress (1993, 2002); **NCV,** *The Holy Bible, New Century Version,* Dallas: Word Publishing, (1987, 1988, 1991); **NIV,** *New International Version of the Bible,* Colorado Springs: International Bible Society (1978, 1984); **NKJV,** *New King James Version of the Bible,* Nashville: Thomas Nelson (1979, 1980, 1982); **NLT,** *Holy Bible,* New Living Translation, Wheaton: Tyndale House (1996).

Published by
LangMarc Publishing
P.O. Box 90488
Austin, Texas 78709
Library of Congress PNC: 2005924006
ISBN: 1-880292-939   USA: $12.95: Can. $16.95

FOR PAL

BARAKA

TABLE OF CONTENTS

Preface

Enjoy Breakfast on the Beach

Breakfast on the Beach: Finding God at the Water's Edge is designed to be your spiritual guide through a seven-day week of worship at the shore. Mornings are the best time to savor each day's selected reading. *Breakfast on the Beach* will get each day off to a great start.

Before You Go...

Before you begin your journey, read "The Beach Before Me." This section will help you prepare for your upcoming adventures at the water's edge.

On the Morning of Your First Full Day...

 Read the chapter entitled "The Sunrise" on the first morning of your visit to the shore. Witnessing the sunrise will enhance this first day's meditation. If you study this chapter in the early morning hours with a cup of your favorite morning beverage at your side, your day and your week will begin in the best way possible. If you miss that early morning quiet time, you can always pack this book in your beach bag and carry it with you to the shore later in the day.

On Your Second Full Day through Your Sixth Full Day...

Approach each day's selection according to the time you have at the beach. If you are staying less than seven days and nights, you might read a chapter at the beginning of the day and another just before bedtime. If you are visiting for just a day or two, this entire guide is brief enough that you can enjoy all nine chapters in an hour or two of quiet time.

On the Evening of Your Last Full Day...

The best time to read the chapter entitled, "The Sunset" is in the early twilight hours of the evening on your last full day at the ocean's edge.

On the Morning of Your Departure...

The final chapter entitled "The Beach at My Back" is meant to be read on the day of your departure, while traveling, or after you have arrived safely back home. Enjoy!

"Just as day was breaking, Jesus stood on the shore...Jesus said to them, 'Come and have breakfast.'"

John 21:4a. 12a (ESV)

"To fall in love with God is
    the greatest of all romances!
To seek Him is the greatest of all
    adventures!
To find Him is the greatest
    human achievement."

—Raphael Simon

INTRODUCTION:
THE BEACH BEFORE ME

"Sing to the Lord a new song, His praise from the ends of the earth, you who go down to the sea, and all that is in it, you islands, and all who live in them."

Isaiah 42:10 (NIV)

"Instead of complaining that God has hidden Himself, you should give Him thanks for having revealed so much of Himself."

Blaise Pascal

Jesus loves the beach!

Follow the footsteps of Jesus, and you'll get sand in your shoes. Walk where Jesus walked, and you'll be no stranger to the shore. Abide with the Son, and your skin will be bronze. The reason is simple. Jesus loves the beach, and He wants you to love it, too.

There is no doubt about it. When Jesus began His ministry, He headed for the water's edge. It's no secret that our Savior selected the seaside town of Capernaum as the headwater for the streams of life-giving water that would pour forth from His teaching, His life, and His ministry.

Take a closer look at the ministry of Jesus, and you'll often see Him along the shoreline. He teaches by the sea, (Mark 2:13); He calls His disciples by the sea, (Matthew 4:18,19); He walks on the sea, (Matthew 14:22-27); He calms the sea, (Mark 4:35-41); He catches fish from the sea, (Luke 5:1-11); He commissions by the sea, (John 21:15-17); He sends His disciples from the seashore, (John 21:18-22); and yes, in His resurrection glory, He serves His disciples a bountiful breakfast on the beach by the sea, (John 21:9-14).

God wants to take you to a new place. Leave the familiar fatigue and the cluttered chaos of your not-so-smoothly ticking days. Prepare to pause and commune with your Creator. Discover the water's edge, and see it again for the very first time. Cast your gaze upon the seascape with freshly polished lenses and a refocused vision. Learn how to catch an unforgettable glimpse of the destiny that God has prepared for the rest of your days.

Prepare to spend a week of worship at the water's edge. Dorothea Lange spent her life as a professional photographer. She said, "The camera is an instrument that teaches people how to see without a camera." The pages that follow are your spiritual camera. This guide is filled with spiritual snapshots that will teach you how to see the seascape with a clearer focus and a sharper spiritual clarity.

Breakfast on the Beach is provided to enhance your ability to experience all the sights and sounds of the seascape through spiritual eyes, so you can better visualize the glory of God at the water's edge. Just as a shaded lens shields your eyes from the glare and sharpens your vision, words on these pages will help you to visualize the beach with breathtaking clarity.

The shape of the shoreline may not have changed. But, as you take time to read and meditate, you will change. Your perspective will change. You will recognize the glory of God all around you. As the rays of the sun tan your skin, the complexion of your life will be changed by the sea. You will leave this place with a fresh new perspective, and in the future you will be more observant of the different facets of God's goodness and greatness on your return visits to a seaward vista.

The beach is beckoning. The sun is rising higher in the sky. Winter's grip is dying, and the promise of spring and summer has awakened your hopes for a fresh new season. The cycle of the seasons is a comforting constant.

Our lives are so crowded with the clutter of relentless busyness. Work, school, housework, homework, the yard, the bills, the agendas, the to-do lists, the interruptions, and the headaches have taken their toll. Now is the time to leave behind the clutter that brings fatigue. Journey to a salutary place to experience a fresh new vision of God where the water meets the shore. This is a sacred place because of the spiritual connection it offers.

The sensations of the shore combine to create a symphony for the soul. The music invites you to connect with your Creator God who has fashioned this refreshing and invigorating place. The globe is adorned with thousands of different venues and vantage points, a cornucopia of coastlines, and a bounty of beaches and shorelines from which to choose. Find your favorite place where the water and the land converge. God has placed these boundary lines for a purpose. Enjoy what God has intended for this season and this place in your life.

The pages that follow are more than the random musings of a middle-aged beachcomber. These pages are your sisal sack filled with treasures from the sea.

The Savior who sculpted the seas is the Creator who has crafted you. So whether your journey takes you to the Outer Banks, Kenya's Jadini Beach, the breakers off Maui, or the lakes of Minnesota, Christ is calling you to commune with Him. He is offering something greater than all the seascapes of the world; He is offering an eternal friendship and a continuing companionship that will last throughout eternity. There is divinity that shapes your destiny and guides your footsteps on this earth.

As a conch shell echoes the sound of the sea, the thoughts, meditations, encouragements, conversations, and contemplations in *Breakfast on the Beach* will echo how wonderfully God has crafted this world and how marvelously He has crafted your life to bring Him pleasure. Yes, your time at the shore will offer real refreshment, real relaxation, and a genuine connection with the people around you. Of greater importance, this will be a time to enjoy and reconnect to the Lord's working and presence in your life.

Waterfront Property of the Soul

No matter where you are in proximity to the beach, *Breakfast on the Beach* is your waterfront property of the soul. The most valuable and coveted real estate along the coast is the highly-prized, much sought-after oceanfront or lakefront property. There are a variety of nice-sounding names to describe the lesser vistas at the seashore. They may be called "ocean side," "lake side," "ocean view," or even "ocean access" or "water access," but only "oceanfront" or "waterfront" has the most cherished of all vantage points: an unobstructed access and a direct line of sight to the shoreline. When you are enjoying the comfy confines of waterfront property, you have the best perspective on all the sights and sounds and sensations of the seashore. Nothing blocks or obstructs your view. Without a doubt, this most desired of all seaside locations is by far the most expensive. Direct access and visibility have a hefty price tag.

Breakfast on the Beach will assist you in gaining a glorious, unobstructed, unhindered view of the glory of God and the greatness of the things that He desires to do in your life and your world. Once you have experienced the view from the waterfront property, you will know it is a direct line of sight to the glory of God. Open your eyes, and enjoy the view.

As each new day unfolds, you will discover different facets of God's creation.

Uncharted Waters

You are embarking upon an exhilarating journey. The beach is more than a place for sunburns, surfing, and seafood. The beach is a place to grow. It is a place to expand your vision of the world and your place in it. Open your heart, and you'll feel the love of God envelope these easy days. Open your hands, and you will receive blessed treasures during your spiritual sojourn at the boundary of the sea.

Like an explorer journeying into exciting, uncharted territory, you will need a compass and a journal to record your daily discoveries. Your compass is the Word of God. Your daily journal at the end of each chapter is divided into four sections. Each section will provide you with thought-provoking questions that will help reveal to you the insights that God has shown you.

The first journal section is **"A Sight to See."** The question asks, "What is God showing me today?" Open your eyes, and you will see the glory of God's good creation.

The second journal section, **"A Shell to Save,"** poses the question, "What truth is God teaching me today?" Open your mind, and you will better understand how God's revelation (His Word) can change the way you live your life.

The third section is **"A Wave to Watch."** A question to consider is, "What circumstances are affecting my life today?"

The fourth journal section is called **"Footprints to Follow."** The question here is, "How is this day going to change the way I live?" Let these queries gently guide your heart and life, and then God's good creation and the power of His word will authenticate His truth in your life and your circumstances.

These journal pages will serve as your own personal "Captain's Log" to record your thoughts, insights, inspirations, and, yes, the connection you make with your Creator as you experience your days by the sea. Use these pages as you choose. They are a simple reminder to make the most of every day you spend at the shore.

Whether you spread your blanket on the sand for a few fleeting moments or stake your claim on the beachhead for several days, let these pages become your trusted companion by the sea. God desires for you to hear His voice above the sound of the crashing waves.

 ## *Selah* by the Seashore

Each chapter closes with one simple, soothing word. The word is *Selah*. In the vocabulary of faith, *Selah* is a mysterious word used only rarely by the writers of scripture; yet beneath the mystery, there is rich meaning.

What are we to make of this mystical and elusive word? Quite literally, the word *Selah* was used as a musical or choir notation that signaled a pause in the music. It means to "pause, reflect, and to consider what has come before." It is like a spiritual speed bump nudging us to slow down and take a break; pause long enough to ponder the truths that have just been proclaimed. *Selah* may be the poet's perfect reflection of Psalm 46:10a, "Be still and know that I am God." (NIV)

Selah is the silence in the midst of the symphony, a wonderful moment to let the music soak into your soul. Your experiences by the sea are intended by God to be a living and breathing *Selah* for your soul.

The beach is before you. Your Creator and His magnificent creation await your arrival. The long, exhausting night is almost over; and the eastern sky is beginning to brighten. The water's edge is drawing near.

Look to the sunrise and let the brilliance of the dawn begin to melt away the darkened dreariness of your tired body and soul.

It is the first day of a new beginning. Get ready to receive all that God has purposed for your life in this sacred season by the sea.

Welcome to the water's edge! Welcome to the new beginning God has prepared and purposed for your life.

Breakfast is served.

Selah…

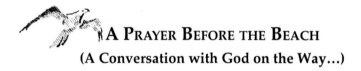

A PRAYER BEFORE THE BEACH
(A Conversation with God on the Way...)

Gracious God, I thank You for giving me this opportunity to journey to the water's edge. As I make my way to the shore that You've prepared and provided, help me to see this as a journey not just to the water's edge, but a journey back into the loving arms of Your glorious presence. Give me fresh eyes to see the splendor of Your creation. Let me rest, and give me the gift of childlike play. Help me rediscover that the greatest joys and the best experiences are getting to know You better.

Loving Lord, I want to feel the fresh touch of Your presence and the comforting reassurance that You are close beside me through all my experiences and adventures that await me at the shore.

Gentle Father, I pray that, when my time by the sea is over, I can return to my home with a better understanding of Your perfect will and Your wonderful way for the rest of my life. I pray this prayer with a real sense of expectation because I claim it in the name of Your Son, my Savior, the risen Christ. Amen.

THE FIRST DAY:
THE SUNRISE

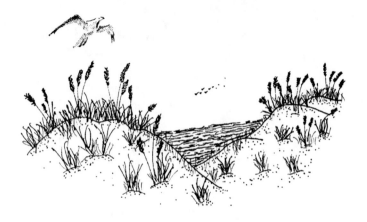

"The path of the righteous is like the first gleam of dawn, shining ever brighter till the full light of day."

Proverbs 4:18 (NIV)

~

"It is right that you should begin again each day. There is no better way to finish the spiritual life than to be ever beginning."
—St. Francis of Sales

The Savior is serving a breakfast banquet by the sea!

The breakfast that Christ has prepared is not made up of the table scraps of religion learned by rote or the false hopes of an often-told distant rumor. The Savior has prepared a banquet table, an abundant feast, a sweet, satisfying friendship with Him. It's a banquet that satisfies our heart hunger to know Him. It is a relationship that can begin now. It is an eternal friendship that He alone has made possible. The breakfast that He has prepared provides a companionship that will outlive the sea.

Begin this new day with a hearty breakfast, a breakfast like none other, a breakfast to be savored by the sea. As the crisp morning air caresses your face, prepare to enjoy a bountiful beachfront breakfast served to you personally by the Lord of Creation. He desires nothing more than to serve you and satisfy the deepest hungers of your heart. What a way to start the day!

As this wonderful new day breaks, sit down and enjoy the meal. What He did in the disciples' lives at the water's edge, He desires to do in your life as well.

A Breakfast on the Beach

Jesus was alive! He had risen from the dead. And despite their doubts and fears, his disciples had seen Him alive. Then Jesus intentionally slipped away. Suddenly, He was gone from their midst. There was a pause in the narrative, a break in the action. *What are we supposed to do now?* they probably were thinking to themselves. Waiting had never been a highly valued commodity to the disciples. No one with the juices of accomplishment coursing through their veins likes to idle their time away.

Peter was no slacker. "When in doubt, do something" was his credo. Headstrong Peter was definitely a man of action. Peter knew, or thought he knew, how to catch fish for a living. While still not quite grasping the reality of the resurrection and its implications for the rest of his life, Peter did the one thing he felt comfortable doing. He decided to go fishing. Thomas, Nathaniel, and the "sons of thunder," James and John, decided to tag along. John records that this impromptu fishing expedition was an abysmal failure. *"...They went out, and got into the boat; and that night they caught nothing,"* (John 21:3).

These were moments of confusion, frustration, and disappointment. Then Jesus arrived at exactly the right moment. Verse four says, *"But when the day was now breaking, Jesus stood on the beach; yet the disciples did not know that it was Jesus."* These untrained, uneducated fishermen were about to make an amazing discovery. They would hear His voice, and they would see His face. Jesus would provide for them in an extraordinary way; He would serve them a magnificent breakfast on the beach; and He wants to do the same for you.

It does not matter how frustrating your life has been up to this moment. Whether your life has been fantastic or a never-ending series of frustrations, you can begin again. You can experience the exhilaration of a fresh start to this new day and to the rest of your life! Do you want to know why? It is because the Lord of creation has sent His sun once again to shine upon your life. Jesus is there waiting for you to acknowledge His presence. He wants to satisfy your deepest longings for relationship, meaning, and purpose in your life. It's time to enjoy His breakfast banquet on the beach.

The First Light

A new day is being born. God is graciously giving you a fresh start.

The darkness is reluctantly relinquishing its strangle-hold on the horizon. The transformation is beginning slowly, almost unseen to the naked eye; yet it is embracing the circle of the earth. The change is total as it encompasses all visible reality. From the depths of the darkness come the first fragile moments of hope for the new beginning of a new day. You grasp that first glimpse of a breathtaking change that is transforming the horizon. The dark of night is fading into the past. Slowly, almost imperceptibly, the darkness is beginning to die even as the light is growing steadily stronger.

As the brightness takes command of the horizon at the infancy of the dawn, something marvelous is taking place. A fresh new beginning is taking in its first breath of salty, morning air. From the vantage point of an eastern shore, the sun rises slowly out of the midst of the sea with all its fire and burning bravado. Your mind knows that the sun has not been submerged in a womb of water, but you see the delivery with your own eyes.

The sun isn't literally rising out of the midst of the waves, but it seems to be born from the briny depths. This ball of fire at the center of our solar system begins to assert its dominion. The fire of hope is kindled in your heart. You begin to consider the possibility for a better today. You begin to dream; "Can I begin again? Can this day be better than the past?" Keep your eye on the morning sky, and watch the pageantry unfold through the morning mist.

You will find your answers as the bleakness of the night retreats. The horizon is transformed with a brightness that brings clarity to your questions.

The shoreline appears to be smiling as the sun peeks above the horizon, and the beach embraces the return of its blazing companion like lovers rendezvousing on a deserted shore.

It is invigorating beyond description to be at the edge of the water when the sun rises, as it has been doing since the first days of creation. *"Then God said, 'Let there be light'; and there was light,"* (Genesis 1:3). The sunrise is a magnificent reminder of the greatness and goodness of God. He has created this incredibly intricate universe. He has marked its boundaries; and He has set its eternal course.

God chooses to reveal Himself in the brilliance and radiance of light. The outpouring of His *Shekinah* glory embarrasses even the brightest star. As you sit on the shore and visually embrace the rising of the sun, you are witness to the faithfulness of a holy God. He is the one who has commanded His sun, and He is the one who is bringing forth the beginning of a grand new day. The majesty of the sunrise reflects a multitude of God's eternal attributes.

God is light, and in Him there is no darkness at all. Those who choose to follow Him live and walk on illuminated paths. *"...the path of the righteous is like the light of dawn, that shines brighter and brighter until the full day,"* (Proverbs 4:18).

Reflecting His Glory

The dawn declares the splendor of His handiwork. Far more importantly, however, the sunrise is a testament to the glory and greatness of God Himself. It is a clear reflection of His glory that outshines the sun! Our solar system's sun is, by comparison, just a flickering ember on a dying campfire compared to the unapproachable brilliance of God's outshining. The light of the dawn is only a prelude to the eternal light that will envelope heaven for all eternity.

In this moment, our eyesight is clouded as though we squint to see through a frosted window, which is a dim foreshadowing to the time when we will fully experience the glory and grandeur of God's presence. The heavenly Jerusalem is a city that, *"...has no need of the sun or of the moon to shine on it, for the glory of God has illumined it, and its lamp is the Lamb,"* (Rev. 21:23). In that new city, the scriptures proclaim that there will be no night. Darkness, along with our rebellion and sin, will be no more. The Lamb will be our Lamp for all eternity.

Reflecting His Faithfulness

Sunrise shines forth with a shimmering reminder of the consistency and constancy of the Almighty. The chorus cries out, "from the rising of the sun, to the setting of the same the name of the Lord shall be praised." The dawn of the morning is a cathedral. It matters not your tradition or your life's pattern of piety, the rising of the sun over the sea is a beautiful opportunity for you to bask in the fresh, new, unleashing of God's glorious faithfulness. The Psalmist declared, *"For the Lord is good; His lovingkindness is everlasting and His faithfulness to all generations,"* (Psalm 100:5).

Embrace this new morning, and rejoice in the reality of the gift of this time at the water's edge. This is the dawn of a new beginning. It is a new day for the blessings that God wants to work into your life.

As the sun reaches higher into the sky and burns away the chill of the night air, speak to God quietly in prayer and tell Him what He longs to hear from you. Express your love for Him. Confess your dependence upon Him, and celebrate the reality of His eternal faithfulness.

> "The Lord's lovingkindnesses [*mercies*] indeed never cease, for His compassions never fail. They are new every morning; great is Your faithfulness," (Lam. 3:22-23, emphasis added).

As this symphony of sunlight continues with its majestic cacophony of light, the sun finally shows its face. A brilliant orange-red sliver of light breaks the surface of the horizon.

Gently and steadily, the light grows bigger and brighter as more of the circle of the sun comes into view. Now the edges of the clouds glow as if to welcome their partner in this planet's paean to their Creator.

The moment comes when the full circle of the sun is standing on the edge of the ocean where the water meets the sky. A shimmering band of glowing orange flows from the base of the sun across the waters to the shore. The sky is on fire. A new day is ours. In a few moments, the fiery glow of the sun will be far too bright to look upon with the naked eye. Yet in these opening moments of this new day, the sun allows even mere mortals a glimpse of its glory.

William Blake, the British poet and artist, understood the infinite power of the sunrise. He wrote, "When the sun rises, do you not see a round disc of fire somewhat like a guinea? Oh no, no, I see an innumerable company of the heavenly host crying, 'Holy, Holy, Holy is the Lord God Almighty.'"

Sunrise is a brilliant reminder from the Creator that we have been given a sacred gift from the hands of a gracious King. We have been given another day to live, to breathe and to commune with the Almighty. We can love again, sing again, embrace again, and think again; and, yes, we can try again. All of yesterday's defeats are now only a fading memory. Today is a new day, one filled with hope and the promise of a day better than yesterday.

All that has gone before is now history. It is gone forever. Any space for regrets, guilt, or gloating is gone. There is only the "now." This is a new day. As finite, frail, transient human beings, this new day is the precious "present" that has been given to us as a gift from God. No wonder the Psalmist exclaimed, *"This is the day which the Lord has made; Let us rejoice and be glad in it,"* (Psalm 118:24).

This is the moment that God wants you to celebrate. Embrace fully what He has faithfully given to you as a gift of His grace. He is giving you a new day and a new beginning. No matter how difficult or cluttered or ugly your life has been, as you gaze into the fiery glow of the sun's shining strength, unwrap the opportunity that you have been given to begin again.

A Reflection of God's Goodness

Consider just how equitable God is. He is just and fair. He graciously gives the same sunlight to every tribe, and every culture, and every nation, and every people group on the planet—yes, just the same sunlight, the same new day.

It doesn't matter how many mistakes you've made or how many victories you've tallied, He gives His light to all in a brilliant blessing of a new day. Both the sinner and the saint receive equally from the hand of the Lord. Those who the scriptures say "have run to do evil" and those who have lived their lives and sacrificed for the good of others each receive from the Lord's gracious hand. God reminds us, *"...for He causes His sun to rise on the evil and the good,"* (Matthew 5:45).

The sunrise, the sky, the sea, and the shore all join hands together to create your own personal sanctuary. The sea birds are your choir, and the beach is your chancel. Speak of His goodness in the morning. The Psalmist wrote, *"God will help...when morning dawns,"* (Psalm 46:5).

The sunrise showcases the multifaceted character of God. He is faithful. He is good. He is great. The glorious news is that your hope for a new day and a new beginning is not based upon you at all. It has nothing to do with your strength, your wisdom, or your ability. They are but stubble blown away by the ocean breeze. Your hope is based upon the awe-inspiring character of God. Let the beach and waves hear your voice echoing your devotion to the author of your hope and confidence for a new beginning.

Open your heart and life with a fresh new allegiance to the glorious God who has brought you to these moments of communion at the edge of the sea.

It is daybreak—sunrise over the waters! Welcome your new day as a fresh new beginning, a grace gift from an eternally good, glorious, and always faithful God who provides for you at the water's edge.

Selah...

 ## A PRAYER AT SUNRISE

Bright and Morning Star, I thank You for the glorious new day that You've ushered in with Your magnificent sunrise. You alone have given me and this world the gracious gift of a new day and a fresh beginning. Because You are the author of this day, I will rejoice and be glad in it. You have watched over me through the darkness of the night, and You alone have brought me into the threshold of this new moment.

Empower me to make the most of this new time in my life. Help me to understand that I can't change the events of yesterday, and help me to move beyond the defeats and hurts of the past. Help me not to squander my thoughts and my time on what might have been. Grant me wisdom to treasure the tomorrows of my life. Liberate me to live in the "now" of this new day.

Give me a fresh vision to see Your hand working in all areas of my life for my good, and let me heed Your call to me for Your eternal purposes. I look forward to knowing You better and loving You even more before this day is done. I pray this confidently in the name of my Savior and Lord, Jesus Christ. Amen.

First Day Journal

"And then God answered: 'Write this. Write what you see..." (Habakkuk 2:2—*The Message*)

I. A Sight To See: What is God showing me today?

II. A Shell to Save: What truth(s) is God teaching me today?

"We are called to an everlasting preoccupation with God."
—A.W. Tozer

III. A Wave to Watch: What circumstances are affecting my life today?

IV. Footprints to Follow: How is this day going to change the way I live?

*"This day is a jewel, sparkling in the light
of a new beginning."*

THE SECOND DAY: THE SEA

*"For the earth will be filled with the knowledge
of the glory of the Lord, as the waters cover the sea."*
Habakkuk 2:14

~

"The infinity of God is not mysterious, it is only unfathomable—not concealed, but incomprehensible. It is a clear infinity—the darkness of the pure, unsearchable sea."

—John Ruskin

The vast, unfathomable sea is a feast for the eyes.

Cast your gaze upon the waters, listen to the waves, and something very sacred is evoked from the deepest part of your soul. Mind, body, and emotions instinctively respond. You are savoring a foretaste of eternity.

The sea welcomes you into the shining, shimmering presence of the eternal One who is responsible for creating it all. J.B. Phillips said, "There is a hint of the everlasting in the vastness of the sea." The waters give testimony that God has been at work in this place.

Boundless Love

The horizon is a happy marriage of sea and sky. Its beauty is only a foretaste of the limitless love of God. *"...I have loved you with an everlasting love..."* is God's message across the ages, (Jeremiah 31:3b).

Praise Him aloud for His limitless love...

"Could we with ink the ocean fill,
And were the heav'ns of parchment made,
Were every stalk on earth a quill,
And every man a scribe by trade,
To write the love of God above
Would drain the ocean dry,

Nor could the scroll contain the whole,
Though stretch'd from sky to sky."

—Chaldee Ode[1]

From the highest dune, you can observe miles of open ocean. Yet, all that you can see from the shore is an infinitesimal sliver of the ocean's magnitude. God's love is vaster than the ocean. The strongest beam of light from the tallest lighthouse can pierce only a paltry twelve miles into the murkiness of the ocean's midnight. It is a captivating sight, but God's love is piercing through the darkness for you.

The Morning Stars Sang

Job was a man overwhelmed by unimaginable pain and loss. In the midst of his own questions and even more questionable friends, God spoke. When the Creator revealed Himself to the created, He raised His righteous right hand and pulled back the veil to display the lavish panorama of His exceedingly good creation.

God asked Job a simple and profound question, *"Where were you when I laid the foundation of the earth?"* (Job 38:4a). He is asking you the same question. When God asked the question, only He could provide a completely satisfying answer.

> "Or who enclosed the sea with doors when, bursting forth, it went out from the womb; when I made a cloud its garment and thick darkness its swaddling band, and I placed boundaries on it and set a bolt and doors, and I said, 'Thus far you shall come, but no farther; and here shall your proud waves stop'?" (Job 38:8-11).

As you stand where the proud waves cease, you are at the edge of eternity, and the testimony of the scenery gives praise to the Creator. All of the magnificence of the ocean's edge echoes a doxology to the grand Designer behind this grand design. The Psalmist declared, *"By the word of the Lord the heavens were made, and by the breath of His mouth all their host. He gathers the waters of the sea together as a heap; he lays up the deeps in storehouses,"* (Psalm 33:6, 7).

We live our lives, for better or worse, in a mostly artificial, man-made, contrived environment. We live controlled lives in controllable spaces and acclimatized artificial atmospheres. When we journey to the sea, we are profoundly confronted with another world quite unlike our workaday routine. It is a wondrous celebration and all five senses are invited. The expanse of the horizon is completely natural. The majesty of the seascape is pure and clean and often without any trace of the artificial.

While we may try to put our man-made imprint on the sea, it is basically untouched. It is unmanageable by the trite dictates of man. Our attempts to change God's creation have been feeble. The sea has submissively and surely obeyed the boundaries set ages ago by the Creator Himself.

"'Do you not fear me?' declares the Lord. 'Do you not tremble in My presence? For I have placed the sand as a boundary for the sea, an eternal decree, so it cannot cross over it. Though the waves toss, yet they cannot prevail; though they roar, yet they cannot cross over it,'" (Jeremiah 5:22).

God is asking you to step aside from your questions and your pain and to consider who He is.

A return to the sea is a return home. It is a return to the very first days of creation and into the very presence of the Almighty Creator God.

"Then God said, 'Let the waters below the heavens be gathered into one place, and let the dry land appear'; and it was so. "God called the dry land earth, and the gathering of the waters He called seas; and God saw that it was good," (Genesis 1:9, 10).

With your eye to the ocean's horizon where the sky touches the sea, your transience on this planet is accentuated.

Mankind is a naturally prideful, self-centered entity. Man has fallen and chosen the path of sinfulness, an outward rebellion from the Creator/God. The ocean is both comforting and unsettling at the same instant. The changeless sea comforts us by its reflection of the Creator's magnificent handiwork. It unsettles us with its ability to shrink our egos. The majesty of the sea calls us to a fresh humility before a glorious God.

When you look at the awe-inspiring immensity of the ocean, you are confronted by the power of the God who created it all with just a word. An undeniable corollary to the handiwork of God is that you are a part of His good creation. There is real significance to your life. You are here for a reason.

Consider the spiritual implications of this thought— God has made your life with the same degree of creative genius with which He has sculpted the seascapes of the globe. Just like the beauty of the beach, your life is the masterstroke of His marvelous masterpiece.

The words of the Psalmist resonate with the exceeding value and worth of your existence:

> "For You formed my inward parts;
> You wove me in my mother's womb.
> I will give thanks to You, for I am fearfully and
>   wonderfully made;
> Wonderful are Your works, and my soul knows it
>   very well.
> My frame was not hidden from You, when I was
>   made in secret,
> And skillfully wrought in the depths of the earth;
> Your eyes have seen my unformed substance;
> And in Your book were all written the days that
>   were ordained for me,
> When as yet there was not one of them."
>   (Psalm 139:13-16)

How big is your God? The prophet Isaiah powerfully posed this rhetorical query:

"Who has measured the waters in the hollow of His hand, and marked off the heavens by the span, and calculated the dust of the earth by the measure, and weighed the mountains in a balance and the hills in a pair of scales?" (Isaiah 40:12).

Imagine if you can, every drop of rain, every puddle, every pond, every drop of ground water, every stream, every creek, every river and lake, and every drop of every ocean and sea. God cradles it all in the hollow of His hand!

Changeless and Ever Changing

The sea is a marvelous mixture of realities. It is calm and still; and, yet, it is always restless. The sea is always the same, yet it is always different. Constantly swirling and shifting, it is a moving mix of momentum and motion. In the twinkling of an eye, the sea that you gazed at only a moment before has already changed. The water has moved and the waves and currents have forever altered the shape of the sea. Astronaut Frank Borman bears witness, "The more we learn about the wonders of our universe, the more clearly we are going to perceive the hand of God."

The restlessness of the sea reflects the nature of your own existence. You crave constancy in an ever-changing world. You can't stop the ticking of the clock, and life doesn't stand still for anyone. You look into the faces of precious young children and know that they will not be young and innocent for long. They'll continue to grow and change, with or without your approval. You are haunted by the ever-increasing fear that one day they'll be teenagers and then (hopefully) responsible adults.

Even your own body betrays you. The eyes that once were 20/20 now can't read the simplest label without the deprecating assistance of reading glasses.

Amid the vacillations and vicissitudes of life, God invites you to experience His glorious and steady guidance. God reveals His constant love and care in the midst of the ever-changing sea tide of our lives. He alone is the One who is eternally the same, yesterday, today, and forever.

The Warmth of the Womb

The mind is at rest at the seashore. The motion of the sea calms your troubled thoughts and emotions as it brings a soothing relaxation to your mind and spirit. This baptism by seaside stimuli brings an almost hypnotic sense of calm.

Perhaps the sound and the rhythms of the waves remind you of the warmth and security that you felt inside your mother's womb. The magnitude of the sea in its size and its depth becomes an all-consuming reality. Kate Chopin has said, "The voice of the sea speaks to the soul."

To stand at the water's edge and look upon its beauty and majesty is to come face to face with the glory of God's great creation and to be welcomed into His presence. Just imagine, the great God who has fashioned this incredibly intricate world is the same Lord who has chosen to reveal Himself to human beings like you and me.

A Beautiful Blue Marble

God has positioned the tiny, spinning orb of earth with miraculous precision. The vast oceans and seas bear witness to the pinpoint positioning of this tiny planet in the midst of the cosmos. God is altogether glorious, and the design of His creation bears witness to His character.

In the parade of uninhabitable planets, the earth is perfectly positioned in the blackness of space. From their astronomical viewpoint, our astronauts have looked back at the earth only to describe it as "the beautiful blue marble" spinning in space. Three-fourths of the earth's surface is covered with water. The Lord of creation has crafted this planet complete with 312,000 miles of seacoast, enough to circle the equator a dozen times.

Everything is present that is needed to sustain life—an overabundance of life. As passengers on planet earth, we are unique in the universe. With the most sophisticated telescopes, scientists have looked into the deepest reaches of the universe and have yet to observe anything that even comes close to replicating the resplendence of planet earth. What a glorious creation! What a glorious Creator!

All of the marvelously complex pieces of information about this planet meld together to give you an even greater reason to commune with and celebrate the One who is responsible for crafting it all.

Habakkuk, the prophet/poet who lived six centuries before the time of Christ, saw into the distant future and described an awe-inspiring future. *"For the earth will be filled with the knowledge of the glory of the Lord, as the waters cover the sea,"* (Hab. 2:14).

God is indescribably glorious and infinitely beyond our frail ability to comprehend who He is. Moses asked of God, *"I pray You, show me Your glory!"* (Exodus 33:18). God gave His answer, *"...I Myself will make all My goodness pass before you, and will proclaim the name of the Lord before you...You cannot see My face, for no man can see Me and live!"* (Exodus 33:19, 20). The Scriptures record that God placed Moses in the cleft of the rock and covered him with His hand while His glory was passing by. Moses saw God's back and that was enough to make Moses' face shine with the reflected radiance of God's glory.

Rejoice and be glad because there is a day coming soon when everyone can and will comprehend His glory. You will experience and have an intimate personal knowledge of the glory of God. The conscious awareness of God's glory will someday cover the earth like the waters now blanket the sea.

Selah…

A Sea Prayer

Lord of the sea and Creator of the universe, as I look out into the unfathomable reaches of the sea, help me to see beyond the horizon of my limited perspective and open my eyes to see more of You and Your greatness. You alone have set the boundaries for the sea, and You have marvelously marked the limits of my life. Teach me to understand a little bit more of Your limitless love for me.

Thank You for creating me just as you have fashioned the wonders of the sea. Calm my anxious heart and help my mind be at rest. Let me know the contentment and fulfillment that only comes in a personal, intimate love relationship with You.

You alone have created this lovely blue marble spinning in space. I look at this world covered with water, and I celebrate Your great creation. I rejoice in the way that You have made me unique among all the billions of people that You have placed on this planet. Help me to know and fulfill the divine destiny and purpose that You have designed for my life. Speed the day when Your glory will cover the earth like the waters now cover the sea. Show me your glory.

I pray all these things in the strong and mighty name of Jesus Christ. Amen.

SECOND DAY JOURNAL

"And then God answered: 'Write this. Write what you see...'" (Habakkuk 2:2—*The Message*)

I. A Sight To See: What is God showing me today?

II. A Shell to Save: What truth(s) is God teaching me today?

"I am a single drop; how can it be that God, the whole ocean, flows into me?"—Angelus Silesius

III. A Wave to Watch: "What circumstances are affecting my life today?"

IV. Footprints to Follow: "How is this day going to change the way I live?"

"Relying on God has to begin all over again every day as if nothing had yet been done." —C. S. Lewis

THE THIRD DAY:
THE SAND

"How precious to me are Your thoughts, O God! How vast is the sum of them! Were I to count them, they would outnumber the grains of sand..."
Psalm 139:17,18a (NIV)

~

"My life is like a stroll upon the beach, as near to the ocean's edge as I can go."
—Henry David Thoreau

The sand is God's sentry.

Stationed on the shore like watchful soldiers, the grains of sand have been commissioned by our Creator to guard the ends of the earth.

"'Do you not fear Me?' declares the Lord. 'Do you not tremble in My presence? For I have placed the sand as a boundary for the sea, an eternal decree, so it cannot cross over it. Though the waves toss, yet they cannot prevail; though they roar, yet they cannot cross over it,'" (Jeremiah 5:22).

Walk in the soft, wind-sifted sand, and let it caress your bare feet. It's a soothing sensation to your weary soles now freed from those suffocating shoes.

Sand bears testimony to both the blessings and the instabilities of this life. It is delightful and it is dreadful. It's delightful as you stroll along the shore, but it's despicable on your kitchen floor. One tiny grain of sand in the eye causes tears, but grains of sand on the beach combine to create a sense of wonder.

The sand is cool and comfortable to walk on until the sun bakes it to the point that it will burn your tender, bare feet. Walking through deep, fluffy sand is an adventure in and of itself. You can lie on the beach, and the sand will conform to the contours of your body.

The sand is never the same on any two beaches. On some beaches, it is soft and inviting; and on other shores, it is coarse and gritty. In some places, God has directed the waves to dredge up piles of rough rocks to be polished into dunes of silky smoothness. In other locales, it appears that God has measured out the powdery white grains and generously blanketed the shore with confectionery sugar.

Best of all, sand offers you an invitation to return to the days of a carefree childhood. The sand of the seashore allows you the opportunity to defiantly discard the so-called dignities of adulthood and return to a simpler time of pure, uncomplicated play. As an adult, you have learned how to work, and your body reminds you of your limitations. A stiff body and aching muscles persuade you that there must be a good reason and a good result for any expended energy. The efficiencies of your purpose-driven life cause you to forget how to pause long enough to play.

The billowing mounds of sand invite the best kind of play. There is mindless fun nestled in the tiny particles. Little pieces of earth, stone, and shell have been polished and pulverized into this marvelous powder. It can now be shaped, molded, thrown, held, piled, and scooped with a shovel. Hold it in your hands. Let it tickle your toes. Let go of that stifling seriousness that afflicts you and discover again the pure laughter of a child at play.

I watched in amazement as my four-year-old son experienced complete bliss by standing in the surf, passionately scooping up handfuls of sand and flinging them into the onrushing surf. Did he think his tiny handfuls would be sufficient to stop the mighty march of these powerful breakers against the shore? Or was he just having fun as only a four year old can? Let the wind and the waves, the sand and the surf be your teachers. Learn to laugh again.

An Abundance Here and Beyond

How much sand is on the seashore? How many grains are there on every beach, every shoreline, and every desert on planet earth? Scientists say that a cubic centimeter (that's a box smaller than a sewing thimble) contains more than 8,000 grains of sand. Mathematicians calculate that the total number of sand grains on planet earth exceeds seven sextillion. That's a seven followed by 21 zeros. It's a magnitude of unimaginable proportions. The human mind can count zeros, but it can never fathom the incalculable grandeur of God's extravagance.

The superabundance of the sand reveals the gracious God who desires to favor His people. The sand is God's servant sent to show us the height, the width, and the depth of the infinite immensity of His love and affection for us.

The beach is a place to experience the extravagant blessings of God. Sand has often been used as an illustration of prosperity and bountiful blessing. When God made His covenant promise to the aged Abraham, God painted the image of a starry sky and a sandy seascape in the patriarch's mind. God wanted the old man to be able to visualize a future filled with abundance for his descendants. Even as the angel stayed Abraham's hand from slaying his son Isaac, God said, *"indeed I will greatly bless you, and I will greatly multiply your seed as the stars of the heavens, and as the sand which is on the seashore...,"* (Genesis 22:17).

When you journey to the edge of the water and dig your feet in the sand, you're experiencing the abundance of God's creation! God blessed Abraham and had a wonderful future prepared for him and his descendants. The God of Abraham has a glorious plan and purpose for your life. Wiggle your toes a little deeper in the soft sand and realize that God is indeed at work in your life. You are exactly where He wants you to be right now.

Acknowledge His handiwork in the midst of His "good" creation.

God promised future blessings for the descendents of David—the man after God's own heart. The prophet Jeremiah may have held a handful of sand heavenward as he spoke the promise of God:

> "As the host of heaven cannot be counted and the sand of the sea cannot be measured, so I will multiply the descendants of David My servant and the Levites who minister to Me," (Jeremiah 33:22).

Jabez was a nobody in a long line of losers, but he dared to ask God for the seemingly impossible, *"Oh, that You would bless me indeed and enlarge my border...,"* (I Chronicles 4:10). Hannah cried out to the Lord in the midst of her heartache and pain, *"...O Lord of hosts, if You will indeed look on the affliction of Your maidservant and remember me...,"* (I Samuel 1:11); and God faithfully remembered her. The dynamic of the doxology found in Ephesians frames your destiny with the One who sculpted the seashore.

> "Now to Him who is able to do far more abundantly beyond all that we ask or think, according to the power that works within us, to Him be the glory in the church and in Christ Jesus to all generations forever and ever. Amen," (Ephesians 3:20, 21).

God often leads His people to strange and new places; places you've never been before. Like an impatient child on a long journey, you sit in the back seat and complain, "How long till we get there?"

There is always the temptation to doubt God's ability to provide for you and to protect you from harm. As God's people journeyed through the wilderness on the way to the Promised Land, the people doubted and they grumbled before the Lord. They wanted food. God gave them manna described by the Psalmist as "the bread of angels;" and, yet, they were still not satisfied. So God sent a mighty wind to blow a bountiful feast of quail for them to enjoy. Again, God provided gloriously beyond all they could ask or hope for. The Psalmist writes, *"When He rained meat upon them like the dust, Even winged fowl like the sand of the seas,"* (Psalm 78:27). Despite their continued legacy of doubt and unbelief, God dramatically showed Himself to be totally trustworthy and dependable.

When God pours His provision into the cup of your life, He is not stingy. The Lord doesn't just fill your life to the rim, He longs to fill your cup to a place of overflowing. That's why King David could honestly say and accurately confess to the greatness of God's provision in his life, *"...my cup runneth over,"* (Psalm 23:5 KJV).

Marvel in the fact that what the Lord has done for Jabez, King David, and His people across the ages is what He desires to do in your life today. Trust Him, yield your desires and wishes to His loving care, and watch how He'll fill your life to a place of overflowing. It can begin today.

Castles of Sand

The beach beckons me to build! The urge to build things out of sand surges within me. The passion to build is as tangible as a conch shell that has washed up on the beach from the ocean depths.

There are people out there somewhere who can come to the beach and truly relax. They can shed every vestige of productivity and not have to achieve or prove anything to anybody. These, I'm sure, are good, strong individuals, wise and thoughtful persons who can lay prone pondering nothing but the seagulls above. Not me, thank you. I want to be building a sandcastle, a granular masterpiece so grandiose that it would make a Frank Lloyd Wright green with envy. Carried away in the adrenaline of the moment, I felt as if my castle creation would stand the test of time like the Pyramids of Egypt. Of course my architectural achievement did not last. The sea has a way of keeping us humble. What I had spent several hours sculpting was gone in the liquid apocalypse of a single spectacular splash.

Kent Keith has written a splendid little book simply entitled *Anyway*. One of his ten paradoxical commandments has particular relevance at the water's edge. He writes, "What you spend years building may be destroyed overnight...build anyway." Keith's insightful commandment is certainly relevant in the time in which we are living. Companies and corporate giants, which have been built and have flourished for decades, are gone in the twinkling of the stock market's eye due to fraud, corruption, mismanagement, or plain old garden-variety greed.

We live in a post 9/11 world. The destruction of World Trade Center Towers has ushered us into a new era. These tall towers were toppled by the worst form of murderous fanaticism and the white-hot hatred that fuels it. Who could have ever imagined that those grandiose pillars of American financial bravado would have come horrifically crashing down in an instant?

My castle didn't really matter much to anyone except me. It was just a matter of time until the waves came and quickly and completely erased my citadel. Within an hour of its completion, there was no trace that it had even existed in the first place. Basking in the soft glow of my own achievement, the waves quickly reminded me of the brevity of my imprint on the shore. I was now straining to find the boundaries of where my edifice once stood.

My experience with sandcastles has not been a tragedy. It has been a delight because it has reminded me, and maybe warned me, of an epic struggle that has been going on for as long as people have left their footprints in the sand.

Perhaps there is something within you that tempts you to strive to make your mark on this world. Deep from within, you may long to leave a legacy. Wars are fought, fence posts are moved, larger buildings are built, and fortunes are grown in hopes that, maybe, someday, somebody will be impressed and, maybe, even remember you after you're gone. You may secretly hope that there will come a day when your likeness will adorn a statue in the middle of the courthouse square to celebrate your accomplishments and exploits. The human experience, at its core, is an unending quest for significance and personal meaning.

Why do you strive for immortality? Why do you believe that the castles you construct or the battles you win will really make a difference? Dwight L. Moody, the great evangelist of the nineteenth century, said it best, "Seeking to perpetuate one's name on earth is like writing on the sand by the seashore; to be perpetual it must be written on eternal shores."

What if, like a castle melting against the rising tide, your best efforts go unrewarded? Your passion for permanence, this inner longing for accomplishment can be the reluctant midwife that gives birth to cynicism and bitterness. A friend who had been scarred by the cutthroat competition of the workplace couldn't help but unleash his bitterness. He bemoaned, "If a man wants to see what kind of impression he's made at work, he ought to stick his hand into a bucket of water and then pull his hand out of the water to see what kind of impression he's left behind." Cynicism has a graceless voice.

This quest for significance has for millennia been the plight of both the great and the small. The white-hot passion to leave a legacy and "make a difference in the world" has continued to be the *Mark of Cain* for countless generations. Multifarious cultures and disjointed generations have joined forces in this legendary quest for greatness. Your best hopes and aspirations are like fearless warriors charging courageously into the oncoming breakers of time hoping that someone will notice that you have passed this way.

No civilization has known the global conquest and the millennium-long military triumph as did ancient Rome. The Caesars and their conquering generals celebrated their epic victories in splendid "triumphal" parades. A slave rode in the chariot holding a golden crown above the head of the hero. While the throngs of Rome cheered and praised their champion, the slave would whisper a warning in the champion's ear, "all glory is fleeting." Listen closely to the slave's whispered warning above all the clamoring noise of your own life that compels you to seek your significance from the sandcastles of your own making. Castle-building is a gently-whispered warning that your earthbound life is temporary.

Jesus talked about sand to prepare you to build a truly lasting legacy, an investment that would outlast the crashing waves of this fleeting existence on planet earth. He simply and directly challenges you to build for eternity.

A Sand Sermon

When Jesus spoke, people listened like never before. Even the fickle crowds knew intuitively that they were hearing the truth. What would it have been like to sit in the sand and listen to His magnificent oration? Jesus' message called "The Sermon on the Mount," recorded in Matthew chapters 5-7, is arguably the greatest single sermon ever recorded. Matthew commented on the crowd's astonished reaction, *"When Jesus had finished these words, the crowds were amazed at His teaching; for He was teaching them as one having authority, and not as their scribes,"* (Matthew 7:28, 29).

Jesus' startling conclusion was a message about building. It was a story of storms and the shifting sands of every life. Jesus commended the wise builder who anchored his house to the bedrock. He had only scathing rebuke to the foolish builder.

"Everyone who hears these words of Mine and does not act on them, will be like a foolish man who built his house on the sand. The rain fell, and the floods came, and the winds blew and slammed against that house; and it fell—and great was its fall," (Matthew 7:26, 27).

With those words of warning, Jesus completed the greatest sermon ever preached.

As you gaze at the location where your castle (real or imaginery) may have stood just a few moments ago, you see only a flat, smooth stretch of beach unmarred by your feeble attempts at architecture. Jesus' praise for the wise builder resonates in your soul, and you are content. You are now free, truly free. The sand and the waves on the beach have graciously freed you from the tyranny of your own self-importance. You are no longer shackled like a slave to your own ego.

The sand has taught you well and set you free to know the truth—the truth that it's not about you, and it's not about me. It is all about the One who created you. You are sand, but He is the rock, the everlasting rock. The Psalmist cried out, *"I love You, O Lord, my strength. The Lord is my rock and my fortress and my deliverer, my God, my rock, in whom I take refuge, my shield…my stronghold,"* (Psalm 18:1, 2).

It is important to build, but it's even more important *where* you build. The sand beneath your feet feels smooth and soft. The sand, in its simplicity, preaches an eloquent sermon. William Blake once wrote, "To see a world in a grain of sand and a heaven in a wild flower, hold infinity in the palm of your hand and eternity in an hour."

For the observant beachcomber, the sand reveals the world, and your hands hold infinity in your palm. Feel the grains of sand between your fingers and toes and remember that they speak volumes of the One who spun this universe into existence. He is the same One who desires to prosper you far beyond your wildest expectations.

Scoop the sand and cradle it in the hollow of your hand. Let it slowly sift through your fingers. Remember that you are but dust; and, yet, you have been fashioned into an eternal soul by the hands of the glorious God of creation. Make sure that the castles you build will stand the test of time. Make every day count for eternity.

The sand still serves as God's sentry keeping watch over the waves. The sand dunes stand guard from the edge of every continent. Just as these stalwart sentries protect the coastline, so the truth of God's Word shields you from the fury of life's storms.

So stroll along the sand as close to the water's edge as you dare.

Selah…

A SAND PRAYER

Loving and merciful Provider and Protector, as I walk in the silky softness of the sand along the sea, remind me today of all your bountiful blessings that You have lavished upon Your people down through the centuries. You have brought me to a place of playful fun. Show me how to throw off the pretense and propriety that I've learned in adulthood, and help me find that place for fun that You want me to enjoy.

Gracious Lord, thank you for this time to enjoy building sandcastles on the beach. At the end of this time of play, help me to avoid wasting time in building sandcastles that won't stand the test of eternity. Guide me in building my life upon the solid rock of Your Word and Your revealed will. Guide me through the shifting sands of my life based upon Your everlasting precepts. Show me Your footprints across the sands of history, and lead me in Your way. *"Teach me Your way, O LORD; and lead me in a straight path,"* (Psalm 27:11 NIV).

Remind me that You are walking with me through all of the experiences of my life. Lead me along life's path and bring me to that place that You are preparing for me.

I pray these things looking to the One who makes my paths straight, my Rock and my Redeemer, the Lord Jesus Christ. Amen.

THIRD DAY JOURNAL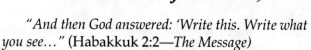

"And then God answered: 'Write this. Write what you see..." (Habakkuk 2:2—*The Message*)

I. **A Sight To See:** "What is God showing me today?"

II. **A Shell to Save:** What truth(s) is God teaching me today?

"I will not just live my life. I will not just spend my life. I will invest my life."—Helen Keller

III. A Wave to Watch: What circumstances are affecting my life today?

IV. Footprints to Follow: How is this day going to change the way I live?

Draw a line in the sand and commit your life, your dreams, and your future to God.

THE FOURTH DAY:
THE SURF

"More than the sounds of many waters, than the mighty breakers of the sea, the Lord on high is mighty."

Psalm 93:4

~

"...If you once get to nature's God, and believe Him, and love Him, it is surprising how easy it is to hear music in the waves, and songs in the wild whisperings of the winds..."
— Charles Spurgeon

Ride the waves! Feel the exhilarating rush of rising above the crushing weight of the water. Move with the unforgiving force of the surf. Experience what only the world's best surfers have known. Master the biggest breakers and imagine yourself "hanging ten" as you soar across the crest of a twelve-foot wave high above the bone-crushing danger below.

The sights and sounds of the surging surf can teach you much about the inevitabilities of life. All manner of circumstances constantly crash onto the beachhead of your life. Fighting these waves leads only to frustration and fatigue. Surf the sea billows that pound against your life, and let the power of the breakers carry you back to the safety of the shore.

Wise Wave Warriors

Watch the waves and learn the lessons that only they can teach. The waves crash into the beach in a never-ending invasion at the edge of the ocean.

Don't ever underestimate the power of the surf. I can remember the enjoyable days of my youth when I would energetically wade out to do battle with the waves. I'd fight the breakers. I would stand firm against the cresting walls of water and attempt to hold my position against their persistent deluge. Time after teeth-rattling time, I would learn my lesson over and over again. In the midst of my stubborn inflexibility, the waves would always win.

As I've grown older and maybe a little more discerning, I'm beginning to understand the surf strategy given to me by a wise and weathered wave warrior. His strategy was simple. "Don't try to fight the waves, you'll never win. Ride the waves instead."

His advice was right on the mark. Though I've never considered myself much of a surfer, the counsel has created a new paradigm in my mind on how to face the things that impact my life. I have a new perspective on the circumstances that reshape my life. Why hadn't I thought of it before? Ride the waves; don't fight them. The art of riding the waves has become a new way of looking at the world. I am now a world-class surfer at work, with my family, and with the people I encounter in everyday life.

There are a wide variety of implements available for riding the surf. There are surfboards, long boards, skim boards, and body boards. I have always been partial to the boards known simply as "boogie boards."

Waves happen. Look at the waves at the edge of the ocean and see that there are forces in this world beyond your ability to control. The waves are always coming. The waves with their pounding, grinding, polishing power are going to find their destiny at the shoreline. Whether you like it or not, whether you accept it or not, and whether you agree with it or not, they come.

Life is a never-ending series of sudden changes and altered landscapes. You can despise these vicissitudes of life or you can learn to ride the waves as they wash ashore. These sudden and unexpected changes of our earthly sojourn are always moving toward you. You must be ready for the pounding the waves bring to your psyche and the polishing they bring to your personality.

The waves can teach you to respect and savor the absolute honesty of God, which is one of the things His people have always appreciated about God and His Word. He never misleads you. He never tries to convince you that the waves will stop pounding on the shoreline of your life. The waves have the power to knock you off your feet. The energy unleashed as the wave breaks can disorient and even disable you. Tumbling and struggling to regain your emotional equilibrium, the waves instruct you with an unrelentingly smack to your mortality and your limitations.

God is honest about the waves. He's always close at hand with a board for you to ride.

The Surf Cometh

Ready or not, the waves keep coming. The edge of the ocean teaches you this unalterable fact of life. Waves, like life experiences, come in all shapes and sizes. Some are huge and overpowering and strong enough to easily sweep you off your feet and push you toward the shore. Others are small and timid and nonthreatening. They tickle your ankles and toes in the sand.

When you are out in the surf, it may seem as if the water is going to totally overwhelm you. Sometimes the painful experiences that wash ashore on the beach of your consciousness can knock down your preconceived notions and your lofty personal proclamations about what life is all about. The Psalmist understood the mighty force of the sea and the intimidating power of the waves. *"Deep calls to deep at the roar of Your waterfalls; all Your breakers and Your waves have gone over me,"* (Psalm 42:7 ESV).

When a large wave hits you, it first lifts you up off the surface of the beach. Your foundation and footing are gone. The weight of your body is suspended between the sand below and the surface of the water above. As the wave moves closer to shore, it reaches a crest and begins to break. Massive amounts of water, hundreds of cubit feet, are moving quickly to the beachhead; and it's very easy to be upended and even flipped over in a whirling motion of the water in the wave. You're disoriented and exhilarated in the same churning instant. It's both frightening and invigorating.

The waves can pack quite a punch when they crest right in front of you. If you can wade or swim or float out far enough into the surf where they haven't yet crested, you can ride the gentle, up-and-down, bobbing motion of the water beneath you. If you go out far enough and still want the security of having your feet planted firmly on the sand beneath you, you'll find yourself having to jump up as each wave goes by to avoid being engulfed by the water. On those particularly hot beach days, the cooling, refreshing, and enjoyable experience of floating along with the motion of the waves as they roll past on their way to their inevitable destination and destiny on the slope of the shore is not such a bad proposition.

The surging surf is a powerful reminder of the way that life unfolds. No sooner than you successfully navigate one wave, here comes another powerful wave. Sometimes before you can even recover from one wave and regain solid footing, along comes another. Before you know it, you're getting a snoot-full of saltwater.

Life is a never-ending series of events and circumstances that keep coming your way. If you are parent, your child's birth comes rolling onto the shore of your life. Then you see the small child waving to you while boarding the bus for the first day of school. Before you can regain your emotional footing, there is a preteen in your household who will claim to possess the Wisdom of Solomon. Be ready for the new waves in your life. The next situation, the next crisis, and the next challenge are all like waves continually washing ashore. You'll waste your time and exhaust your energy trying to fight them.

There's no use being angry about the presence and persistence of the waves in your life. Remember to ride the waves as your teenager climbs behind the wheel of your vehicle and drives off with a driver's license in hand. The first time this teen goes out on a date without a chaperone, you must simply ride the wave. The unrelenting waves in life do keep bashing against you.

Storm Surge

The days are spectacular on the Outer Banks of North Carolina when a tropical storm remains stationary offshore. From a hundred miles away in the open ocean, the storm reaches in to plunder the coastline. The storm's arsenal contains ferocious winds, heightened waves, foam billowing off the crests of the breakers, and the deafening roar like the sound of a thousand waterfalls. The red warning flags wave frantically as they herald their stern warning—"No Swimming!" As the wind pushes the flagpoles nearly to the breaking point, they take an unflinching stand along the beachfront like stalwart soldiers braced against an amphibious invasion. Those folks brave enough to venture out into the overpowering gale must lean hard against the wind.

Hearty hikers wrapped in rustling windbreakers feel a tangible touch of the manifest presence of the Lord of Hosts. The energy revealed in the wind and the waves leaves you awestruck. Line after line of white-capped waves roll into the shore, and they join forces to create an impregnable foaming wall of billowing white water. The roar of the water declares the grandeur of God's greatness. Maybe the psalmist braced himself against the ferocity of the wind and the sea when he wrote, *"More than the sounds of many waters, than the mighty breakers of the sea, the Lord on high is mighty,"* (Psalm 93:4).

In the heart of the storm, the stronger the wind, the higher and fiercer the waves will be. The higher the waves, the more severe the devastation that will be unleashed on the unguarded beach.

Rip Currents of the Heart

The winds were especially strong during a recent visit to the edge of the ocean. The winds were so brisk that the lifeguards had been warning swimmers and surfers of strong and dangerous rip currents. For two consecutive days, the bright red warning flags had been flying. Safety officials had hoped that the threat of a $250 fine might dissuade surfers from taking on the challenge of the ferocious waves strengthened by the nearly gale force winds.

As I've listened to the lifeguards and read the beach brochures, I've learned about rip currents. A rip current is formed when two large masses of water converge at the shore and then flow out together in a thirty-foot wide trough of powerfully flowing water that rushes far out to sea. The undertow from this rip current is strong enough to pull even the strongest swimmer far out into deeper water. The safety of the shoreline is quickly a great distance away.

Being out to sea is serious business, but the worst part is yet to come. The real danger of the rip current occurs when the swimmer, caught in this mighty rush of water, attempts to swim directly into this rip tide. In a worse case scenario, the swimmer tires quickly, is overcome by the force of the water, and reaches a point of physical exhaustion. Pushed far from shore into ever deepening water with no strength left to swim, the potential for drowning becomes more real with each passing second.

There are those dark times in your life when you face rip currents of the heart. Those horrible times when the unspeakable happens with little or no warning. You lose all perspective. The pain of the crisis pushes you away from the certainties of life that you once held close. You are suddenly in unfamiliar territory. You are afraid, and you thrash about trying to find answers and a sense of security. However, these powerful, painful crises in your life, like rip currents, push you into the deep, colder waters of doubt, fear, and uncertainty. You feel lost and alone. You try to fight your way back to shore using your own strength, but with each stroke you feel yourself becoming weaker. Deep within, you sense that you are losing the battle to get back to the beach.

Biblical Wave Riders

Jonah was a land-lubber who learned respect for the waves the hard way. Jonah found himself in the rip current of his own rebellion against God and His clear command on his life. He intentionally turned away from God; literally, he ran away from the responsibility that God had given to him. As a result, God allowed a miraculous series of events to unfold in Jonah's life. All these potential calamities worked together for Jonah's good. The rip tide of his rebellion pushed him to a place of complete spiritual exhaustion. At the end of his own strength, the reluctant prophet repented. Jonah described his desperate situation graphically, *"For You had cast me into the deep, into the heart of the seas, and the current engulfed me. All Your breakers and billows passed over me,"* (Jonah 2:3).

Habakkuk lived a wave-tossed life. He probably wouldn't be offended if you've never taken the time to read the book that bears his name in the Old Testament. Just in case, read it to save yourself a red-faced moment of introduction in heaven. This lesser-known prophet/ poet communicates God's truth in many profound ways. Habakkuk may have never left many footprints in the sand, but he certainly understood the dynamics of the surf. Habakkuk's ministry was to warn God's people of the waves of God's judgment. The waves were about to rush onto the shore of their national life.

Habakkuk knew that the nation of God's people had fallen into deep rebellion and disobedience. He also knew that the tsunami of judgment was coming. Yet in the midst of the madness and the impending judgment of God, he spoke powerfully of God's mercy and forgiveness. He concludes his book with a gut-level honesty that is so characteristic of God's Word to our lives.

> "Though the fig tree should not blossom and there be no fruit on the vines, though the yield of the olive should fail and the fields produce no food, though the flock should be cut off from the fold and there be no cattle in the stalls, yet I will exult in the Lord, I will rejoice in the God of my salvation. The Lord God is my strength, and He has made my feet like hinds' feet, and makes me walk on my high places," (Hab. 3:17-19).

These are some pretty frightening waves. It is a description in no uncertain terms of a complete economic meltdown. For the people of Habakkuk's day, the prophet's message meant people would starve to death. In the midst of these onrushing breakers, Habakkuk rides those waves to a place he describes as *"...my high places,"* (v. 19b). He draws his strength directly from his relationship with the Lord. He uses the word "exult," which is a much stronger form of the word "exalt." "Exult" is the word "exalt" on spiritual steroids. Habakkuk sees the waves of God's judgment coming, and he decides to surf the breakers. The "long board" of his life was his unwavering confidence and trust in the power, justice, and faithfulness of the one true God.

Surviving in the Surf

Just as Jonah and Habakkuk survived the surf and rode the waves that came crashing into their lives, so can you. The experts say that there is a way for the wise swimmer to escape the dangers of the rip current. The key to survival is awareness. The force of the water cannot be defeated. You can't beat the surge of water against you. Ride with the flow of the current rather than against it. The secret to survival is to swim parallel to the shore (at a 90-degree angle to the direction of the wave), not directly back toward the shore (at a 90-degree angle to the beach). From an observer's vantage point on the shore, it would look as if you were swimming down the beach, which is exactly what you'd be doing.

The width of an average rip current is only thirty feet wide. In a matter of moments, you'd be out of the rip current; and you could more easily swim back to the beach with the flow of the water. Incredible! The secret to survival in the surf is swimming with the flow of the water. It's the secret that can save a swimmer's life.

Heartaches and life sorrows will roll into your life when you least expect them. You can't fight *against* these emotional breakers any more than you can tame the tide. If you're not careful, the pain and grief you feel will push you far away from the comforting embrace of God in your life. You'll wake up as if from a nightmare and find that God seems far away.

Much like a rip current, grief and sorrows can separate us from the love of God that we experience in the happier times. We must learn the lesson of the rip current to find our way back to the beach. Go with the flow! See where God is taking you. Never doubt His love and swim in cooperation with the current wherever it may take you. When the time is right, you can begin to feel the flow of the water carrying you back into the arms of a God who loves you and desires to comfort you in the midst of life's darkest hours.

Sorrows like Sea Billows

There was a man named Horatio G. Spafford whose life spanned sixty years during the nineteenth century. He experienced some of life's most crushing blows. As his wife and children were crossing the Atlantic, their ship sank and their lives were lost. Spafford allowed the crushing weight of the grief he felt to carry him out to sea, literally, like a rip current of the heart. Spafford booked passage on a ship sailing the exact course his wife and children had taken. When the ship reached the spot in the ocean where his family had perished, Spafford penned these words to what is now a widely known and dearly beloved hymn of hope entitled "It Is Well with My Soul." The words stand in monument to a man who allowed the pain in his life to carry him to a place of complete trust and an uncompromising confidence in our Savior and God.

The waves are a reminder of the things that will come into your life. The waves are a reassurance of our need to stay close to God. The waves with their mighty roar and punishing power remind you that God controls them and constrains them. *"For He spoke and raised up a stormy wind, which lifted up the waves of the sea,"* (Psalm 107:25). God also is the One who can calm the storm, quiet the winds, still the sea, and turn the roar of the waves into a whisper. *"He caused the storm to be still, so that the waves of the sea were hushed,"* (Psalm 107:29).

In the light of the majesty and the power of the Almighty, the roar of the waves and the sound of the sea against the beach become a comforting and soothing symphony to the Savior who watches over this world and every wave that touches your life.

Selah…

A Surf Prayer

Lord of the waves, calm my heart in the midst of the waves and breakers that are crashing into my life right now. I need Your help to resist the urge to fight the waves and to acknowledge that I can't stop the waves from lashing at the shoreline of my life. Bring the balance into my life that only You can give. Enable me to ride the waves that could cause me to lose my balance and fall. Keep Your steady hand upon my life guiding me in these anxious and troubling moments.

Give me Your eternal perspective in the midst of the rip currents of my heart. Let me gain a better awareness and acceptance of the waves in my life. Bring me back to the safety of Your shore. Teach me to stand even when it seems as if the stuff of this life that is bearing down on me will knock me to the ground.

Loving Lord, when I fall and the breakers wash over me, please lift me up and allow me to have courage in the midst of the crashing waves. I rejoice in the fact that even when I fall seven times, You grab my hand to pull me up.

I am glad that You have the power to calm the waves in my life. Sovereign Lord, advance Your kingdom's purpose in my life. When I see the waves coming toward me and when I hear their deafening roar, I praise You for being the steadying presence in my life today.

I pray these things in the name of the One who walks on the waves and calms the storms, the risen Christ. Amen.

Fourth Day Journal

"And then God answered: 'Write this. Write what you see…"(Habakkuk 2:2—*The Message*)

I. A Sight To See: What is God showing me today?

II. A Shell to Save: What truth(s) is God teaching me today?

"Everything that God brings into our life is directed to one purpose: that we might be conformed to the image of Christ."
—Erwin Lutzer

III. A Wave to Watch: What circumstances are affecting my life today?

IV. Footprints to Follow: How is this day going to change the way I live?

"If you're going through difficult times today, hold steady. It will change soon. If you are experiencing smooth sailing and easy times now, brace yourself. It will change soon. The only thing you can be certain of is change."

—James Dobson

THE FIFTH DAY:
THE SKY

"For Your loving-kindness is great above the heavens, and Your truth reaches to the skies."

Psalm 108:4

~

"What idea could we have of God without the sky?"

— George MacDonald

The sky above you is God's Cathedral.

Never has a craftsman's chisel or a stonemason's marble even come close to reflecting what God did when He unfurled the sky and stretched it out like a canopy over the sea.

The multicolored shades of blue, punctuated with the wisps of white clouds, create a masterpiece in the sky. A heavenly Michelangelo paints this dome above you.

Lift your eyes to the heavens in this quiet cathedral. God is inviting you to do more than fix your eyes upon this hallowed and holy sight. Your eyesight is limited. He is lifting your eyes to raise your vision. Your vision is not a place, a perspective, or even a panoramic view. Your vision is a person. The person is Jesus, the Christ.

God spread out the heavens to reveal Himself. Then He left heaven to set foot on the edge of the sea. He has taken the initiative and come to earth. He has dwelt among us. God became a man. In the original language, the scriptures speak of God "pitching His tent" to live with us on earth. John writes, *"And the Word* [Christ] *became flesh* (human, incarnate) *and tabernacled—fixed His tent of flesh, lived awhile—among us; and we* [actually] *saw His glory—His honor, His majesty; such glory as an only begotten son receives from his father, full of grace* (favor, loving kindness) *and truth,"* (John 1:14, Amplified).

God clothed Himself in human flesh so that He could bring His message of salvation to save mankind from sin. Jesus took great pleasure in standing on the beach, gazing heavenward, and enjoying His exceedingly good creation from an earthbound perspective. The Savior who raised His eyes heavenward wants you to lift your vision to embrace the wonders and mystery of His marvelous creation.

The sky unveils a world of possibilities. The sky is a reminder of the freedom you enjoy. It ministers to your soul an unshackled, unfettered freedom to embrace your dreams, follow your aspirations, and journey farther than you would have dared before. The length and breadth of this dome above the earth becomes your spiritual tutor. It helps you to understand just how majestic God's vision is for your life and your future.

Isaiah admonished the people to lift up their eyes to the heavens in order to catch a fresh glimpse of what God was doing in their world. Lift your gaze heavenward, let your eyes scan the horizon, and try to comprehend the limitless possibilities that God has prepared for you both now and in eternity.

Along the shoreline, your senses are richly fed by the grandeur of the heavens. The sky stretches beyond the mind's ability to comprehend. With your eyes earthbound in the valleys of your everyday gyrations, you often miss God's gracious gift of His outstretched heavens. Lift up your vision and see the Christ, *"For who in the skies is comparable to the Lord? Who among the sons of the mighty is like the Lord?"* (Psalm 89:6).

Claustrophobic Circumstances

There are concrete canyons in this artificial world. The shadows of your superficial surroundings threaten to suffocate you, block your vision, crowd your consciousness, and blind you to the mighty works of God. Nothing disappoints you like the pale regret of a sunset squandered and an opportunity lost to be visually drenched in the brilliance of a summer evening's twilight. God mixes the pigment from His heavenly paint palette to brush the sky with shades of pink, orange, and colors of the rainbow. He saves the gold for the moon peaking over the horizon to gleam over the now-black water.

Missing a sunset carries its own penalty. Even more disheartening is to miss the grandeur of God's gracious activity in your life. Be vigilant so that your crowded schedule will not obscure God's handiwork and block your ability to see the glorious things that God is doing.

Now is a time of cultural claustrophobia. Nothing quenches the human spirit quite like feelings of being "boxed in" and trapped by the societal expectations around you. How often have you heard someone say in desperation, "I need my space!"

The sky answers this clarion call from deep within your heart for a touch of liberating freedom. Allow your hunger for freedom to be satisfied by the unveiled sky.

The credo of our claustrophobic culture is a well-rehearsed cliché, "think outside the box." This meaningless mantra of committee meetings is most often uttered by those attempting to appear adventurous and innovative. But you do not want to just "think" outside the box, you long to *live* outside the box.

Ours is a culture of confined living from birth until death. As a baby you are immediately introduced to a box called a crib. You live your life in a box called a house or an apartment. You travel from place to place in a car, truck, or van, which is basically a box with wheels. You may work in a box, whether it's an office or a confining cubicle; you spend your days earning your wages wedged in four walls. Your life comes to an end, and your body is placed into a box.

Deep within you, you long to be free for at least a few fleeting moments. There is a yearning to live, breathe, and think beyond the boxes imposed upon you by our cloistered culture. Often, the boxes that confine and constrain you are of your own making. Antiquated attitudes or lowered expectations rob you of a vision for a brighter future. You habitually turn your thoughts to the negatives planted by your self-defeating subconscious. You may feel trapped and spend your days wondering if you'll ever be able to break free from the walls that confine and define you. Cast your gaze heavenward and the dream gives way to a promising reality. The sight of the sky refreshes you and proves to be an answer to your soul's cry for freedom and hope.

A Glimpse of Heaven

The human spirit, fashioned in the likeness of the Almighty, longs for the sweet fragrance of freedom and the joys of relationship. From the worst depths of man's inhumanity to man, solitary confinement has been devised as the diabolical assassin of the spirit. While evil men treat each other harshly, God graciously provides those things for which you most desperately yearn. Consider what God has prepared for you in the corridors of eternity.

There will be no claustrophobia in heaven. God's heaven will be a panoramic place, a true wide-screen experience that will defy your preconceived notions and superficial earthly perspective. The expansive heavens above us give a foretaste of our Creator, the glories of His good creation, and a glimpse of our eternal destiny. I Corinthians 2:9 promises, *"Things which eye has not seen and ear has not heard, and which have not entered the heart of man, all that God has prepared for those who love Him."*

Maybe that's why the human soul instinctively responds so joyously to the sight of God's canopy. Like a master painter mixing rich colors, the deep blue of the summer sky mingles with the aquamarine of the water below. There are some days when the sky is so blue and the clouds so white that it almost takes your breath away. The synergy of vivid colors, the pungent aroma, and the soothing sounds at the water's edge refresh and replenish your earthbound soul. This breathtaking beauty is a preview of heaven. The resplendent vistas are a foretaste of a place that will be home.

From A Distance

As Jesus walked along the beach, He lifted His vision heavenward and kept His eyes on the sky. Religious leaders came to the edge of the sea to question (trap) Jesus. He looked up into the brilliant sky and said,

"When it is evening, you say, 'It will be fair weather, for the sky is red.' And in the morning, 'There will be a storm today, for the sky is red and threatening.' Do you know how to discern the appearance of the sky, but cannot discern the signs of the times?" (Matthew 16:2, 3).

Walk with Christ along the sandy shores and discern the signs of the times. The sky shows God's unfolding plan for your life. The sky bears witness to the wisdom of God's redemptive mission.

Stand on the seashore and gaze into the distance. You may see the building of a thunderstorm hours before it arrives. This perspective gives you precious time to prepare for what's ahead. Your personal storms may come with no warning. Life is filled with unexpected experiences that can sneak up on you. Society has become dependent on expensive and sophisticated electronic toys that scan the skies and warn us of approaching storms. Unfortunately, they don't make Doppler radar for the human heart.

What does the sky show you about God's purpose for your future? Even better than the latest radar technology, your Heavenly Father wants you to have "Big-Sky" optimism. The woman described in Proverbs 31 is a person with an unshakable "Big-Sky" outlook on life. *"She is strong and is respected by the people. She looks forward to the future with joy."* (Proverbs 31:25 NCV)

Don't let the ominous clouds of an uncertain future make you afraid. God wants you to live a "Big-Sky" life. Isaiah spoke of the Lord's encircling presence in the lives of His people. *"The Lord will go before you, and the God of Israel will be your rear guard."* (Isaiah 52:12b ESV)

God wants you to have an unshakable confidence as big as the sky at the water's edge. Lift up your eyes and see that God is actively at work in your life. Hear the prophet's voice that echoes God's promise to your life. *"'I say this because I know what I am planning for you,' says the Lord. 'I have good plans for you, not plans to hurt you. I will give you hope and a good future.'"* (Jeremiah 29:11 NCV)

God's Skywriting

The sky is ablaze with God's signature. The heavens declare God's unfolding story written on the canvas of the sky.

From the very beginning of redemptive history, God has etched his story in the heavens. On the second day of creation, God shaped the heavens. *"Then God said, 'Let there be an expanse in the midst of the waters, and let it separate the waters from the waters. God called the expanse heaven…,"* (Genesis 1:6, 8).

Like the depths of the oceans, the sky is a marvel of this physical world that God has created. The vastness of the sky and sea is but another glimpse into the glory and grandeur of God Himself. The sky and sea are the brush strokes of God's self-portrait. Paul underscores this truth in Romans 1:20.

"From the time the world was created, people have seen the earth and sky and all that God made. They can clearly see His invisible qualities—His eternal power and divine nature. So they have no excuse whatever for not knowing God." (Romans 1:20 NLT)

The Psalmist joins this great chorus in praise to God for His marvelous works, *"For Your lovingkindness is great above the heavens, and Your truth reaches to the skies,"* (Psalm 108:4).

God continues His skywriting to this day. Have you seen a rainbow arched over the ocean after a summer thunderstorm? The multicolored bow in the sky is God's reassuring message, repeated down through the ages: He keeps His promises!

When mankind's wickedness had reached its rebellious pinnacle, God's holiness demanded judgment. Divine punishment fell from the sky, and the global deluge that followed is history. Even with His righteous judgment, God remembered mercy. He rescued Noah and his family. God provided an ark of rescue.

When judgment had passed, Noah's family experienced more than a fresh start and a cleansed new world. They were welcomed into a new beginning and a new understanding of the great God of covenant relationship. God's voice was clear and comforting as recorded in Genesis 9:13-15 when He pointed Noah to His skywriting:

"I set My bow in the cloud, and it shall be a sign of a covenant between Me and the earth. It shall come about, when I bring a cloud over the earth, that the bow will be seen in the cloud, and I will remember My covenant, which is between Me and you and every living creature of all flesh..."

A Vision of Victory

Jesus looked into the sky and saw the victory that His death on the cross would bring. Jesus said, *"I saw Satan fall like lightning from heaven,"* (Luke 10:18 NIV).

How could the disciples have known that Jesus' vision of the devil's ultimate defeat would be written in the sky? Satan witnessed the agonizing death of Christ on the cross. Lucifer laughed. The closest followers of Jesus ran away clothed only in their shame and grief. The women wept at the foot of the cross. The weary world waited.

The sky greeted the first glimmers of the sunrise on Sunday morning. The earth shook and the massive stone that blocked the entrance of the tomb moved. The Roman guards were frozen in fear and, risking certain military execution for their desertion, they fled into the morning mist.

The One who had defeated death and the grave first comforted and then commissioned His followers. The Lord of the heavens then rose into the sky and vanished from their sight. Can we blame the disciples for being mesmerized by this miraculous sight? God sent his angelic messengers to give them a new focus. *"...Men of Galilee, why are you standing here staring at the sky? Jesus has been taken away from you into heaven. And someday, just as you saw Him go, He will return!"* (Acts 1:11 NLT).

The sky received the risen Christ into heaven when He ascended, and the sky will present the Christ when He returns.

The sky announces the advance of God's plan and His kingdom. When asked about the circumstances of His return to earth, Jesus clearly warned his disciples that His return would not be limited to only those in close geographical proximity. *"At that time if anyone says to you, `Look, here is the Christ!' or, `Look, there he is!' do not believe it,"* (Mark 13:21 NIV).

Jesus encouraged his followers to look into the sky with a discerning spiritual eyesight.

"At that time men will see the Son of Man coming in clouds with great power and glory. And He will send His angels and gather His elect from the four winds, from the ends of the earth to the ends of the heavens," (Mark 13:26, 27 NIV).

In a dramatic display of God's sovereignty over all of human history, "...*the sun will be darkened, and the moon will not give its light; the stars will fall from the sky, and the heavenly bodies will be shaken,*" (Mark 13:24b-25 NIV). When history reaches its redemptive zenith, the sky will conclude its ministry to a watching world. Scripture records a vision of the future when the sky will be retired. "*The sky receded like a scroll, rolling up...,*" (Revelation 6:14 NIV).

The heavens have told of Him from the days of creation and will continue to bear witness of Him until His "glorious return." The sky has been the canopy of God's creation and the beautiful blue canvas with which He has drawn our eyes toward eternity. The sky beckons you to lift your head and to raise your eyes above your limited and often pessimistic view of current circumstances and the wickedness of the world.

The ancient prophesies that announce the return of the King invite you to look up. "*When these things begin to take place, straighten up and life up your heads, because your redemption is drawing near.*" (Luke 21:28)

As the future unfolds, the sky will one day fold its temporal tent and bow to the supremacy of the Resurrected Christ. The Lord, through His marvelous Word, promises that the sky will be a strategic part of His signs and wonders that reveal His mastery over our individual destinies and the destiny of the nations.

Lie back in the soft, warm sand and cast your gaze into the brilliant blue sky. Enjoy the breathtaking beauty as God has intended. Marvel at God's creation and the goodness of His plan, but remember that the awe-inspiring sky is also a reminder that you are here but for a brief time. Like your frail human body, the sky is on temporary assignment. It is here now only to give testimony to the greatness of the One who created it for your enjoyment and edification. He created it to draw you into a closer and more intimate personal friendship, an everlasting bond with the Lord of creation.

As splendid as the sky and sea are now, the Lord speaks of a time in the future when even their apparent permanence will be revealed to be as fleeting as the morning breeze. Jesus spoke of the transience of the whole created order when He said, *"Heaven and earth will pass away, but My words will not pass away."* (Matthew 24:35).

Selah...

A Sky Prayer

Lord of Heaven, I rejoice that Your glory reaches to the sky! I don't just want to see the physical world with all its beauty and grandeur; I want to see You. Open my eyes that I may see the unlimited qualities of Your love and mercy.

Free me from the claustrophobic perspective of my day-to-day life. Please help me to avoid getting boxed into thinking that You don't see or care. Let me know and come to realize Your unshakable presence in my life here and eternally.

Lord, I love the way You dramatically write in the sky. The rainbow after the summer shower reminds me that no matter how unfaithful I may be, You always keep Your promises. Reveal to me the victories that will follow the storms of my life, and let me enjoy the multi-colored brightness of Your messages to my life.

Savior, I rejoice that my greatest enemy has fallen like lightning from the sky. Thank You for going to the cross to defeat my sin, my death, and my greatest adversary, the devil himself. Thank You for the sky, which has given testimony to the dramatic conquest of Your victory.

Help me to delight in the fact that You will return again for me and those who love You. Lift my eyes heavenward and quicken my heart to expect and look for Your return. I can't wait to see You face-to-face.

It is in great anticipation that I pray all these things in the name of the returning King of Kings and reigning Lord of Lords. Amen.

FIFTH DAY JOURNAL

"And then God answered: 'Write this. Write what you see..." (Habakkuk 2:2—*The Message*)

I. A Sight To See: What is God showing me today?

II. A Shell to Save: What Truth(s) is God teaching me today?

"The universe is centered on neither the earth nor the sun. It is centered on God."—Alfred Noyes

III. A Wave to Watch: What circumstances are affecting my life today?"

IV. Footprints to Follow: How is this day going to change the way I live?

"Worship is a way of living, a way of seeing the world in the light of God…to rise to a higher level of existence, to see the world from the point of view of God."
—Abraham Heschel

THE SIXTH DAY:

THE SHELLS

"…they will feast on the abundance of the seas,
on the treasures hidden in the sand."
Deuteronomy 33:19 (NIV)

~

"One cannot collect all the beautiful shells
on the beach. One can collect only a few, and
they are more beautiful if they are few."
—Anne Morrow Lindbergh

There are treasures buried beneath your feet.

Every shell on the beach is a subtle reminder that God showers His children with surprises of unexpected and undeserved gifts each and every day.

Walk along the edge of the ocean and experience the generosity of the sea. You need not look for the treasures because they will find their way to you. Be patient and wait for them to appear. The beach is a learning center for nurturing a spirit of patience. Linger here and learn to free your life from the scurrying, scratching impatience that robs you of true contentment and gratitude.

The tyranny of our technologies squeezes the virtue of patience from us personally and from our society. The cadence of your workaday life forces you into a frenzied march. Your ears ring with the shrill voices that compete for and demand your immediate and undivided attention. Now the sea whispers in your ears....*wait.* Listen to the sea and remember the serenity of your Savior.

The lessons from our culture can deceive you. You have learned from experience that, if you want what life has to offer, you must work hard for whatever you get.

The edge of the ocean reminds you of the generosity of the sea. Shells are treasures from the depths of the sea.

As you walk along the sandy shore, shells, stones, pebbles, and tiny bits of gravel and rock slide across the slope of the shore to greet you. The variety of shapes and colors reflects the rich tapestry of living things that reside in the sea. When the tide retreats, the waves reveal a world of hidden treasures.

Every shell has a tale to tell and offers a glimpse of the ocean's story. For many a sea creature, the tiny shell that you now hold in your hands is a relic of a life lived long ago. Each shell has served as a home and a shelter from the storms. Like the conch shell that echoes the sound of the sea, the shells ring out their story. Listen closely and maybe you'll hear the faint echo of swash-buckling songs from the Spanish Main. Close your eyes, and you might hear parrots in tropical trees telling stories of fishes and sea horses deep beneath the sea. Yes, every shell has a story to tell, tales that only they know.

These aquatic residents have long since left the comfortable confines of the shells. Whether their lives ended or they moved up into more spacious accommodations, all that remains is an empty shell.

The intricacy of each shell's design has the fingerprints of our Creator! These simple life-forms are seemingly inferior to the rich complexity of your human body. Even at a simplistic level, the shells speak of a perfect design.

On this sun-washed day by the sea, the shells are the stuff of great collections. Long after you've bid this glorious place a begrudging good-bye, these treasures from the sea will revive the joy you have known at the edge of the water. These are the relics of a relationship that you have formed with the sea.

Shell fragments have been pounded and sanded by the waves until all the rough edges and coarse designs have melted into an incredibly smooth surface. Occasionally, a shard of glass is transformed by the crushing, churning, polishing power of the waves and the water. What a thrill it is to find a piece of glass on the shore. Only a short time ago, this sharp, piercing sliver of glass in search of a bare foot would have been an item of dread. The ocean has done its work, and there's no longer any reason to fear this once sharp bayonet; the glass sliver is dangerous no more. Now it is a delightful reminder of the softening wonder of the water.

This mix of water and waves, sea and sand are performing the same miracle for wearied psyches. They conspire together to smooth the rough edges of your soul. Were you becoming like that once sharp and menacing piece of glass? Were you a danger to the tender sensibilities of someone who might cross your irritable path? Has the sea begun to do its sanding and polishing work in your life? Has the rhythm of the waves now caused you to become a more gracious person?

As you hold the now smooth and pleasing piece of beach artwork in your hand, you are beginning to understand that God is using the elements of His exceedingly good creation to mold you into a more introspective and considerate person.

Think of your existence on this tiny planet and how infinitesimally small you are in comparison to the God who has fixed the planets in their orbits. There is much less distance between you and the tiny sea creatures that once inhabited the shell in your hand than there is in the infinite gulf that exists among you, the creation, and the Almighty Creator.

If God has so wired you that you can derive joy from a tiny shell or stone, surely, you are reminded that an awesome God also takes delight in you. Imagine that! In spite of your weaknesses, limitations, and frailties, the Creator of the universe delights in *you*.

The shells are the learned professors and the seashore is the lecture hall. If you are attentive to their living lectures, you can learn of the things that really matter in this life and the life to come. The shells are gentle reminders to slow down. Allow God to smooth you and polish you. He holds you in His hand and delights in you.

The Shell Seeker

On a recent retreat by the sea, I began a collection of shells. Like a battle-hardened buccaneer searching for buried treasure, my stroll along the shore became an eagle-eyed quest for that perfectly sculpted shell, which I could triumphantly add to my treasured collection.

The shells are teaching you to wait. They are a reminder that the good things, the truly precious things in life, are worth waiting for. They transport you to the daybreak of faith. Your fellowman is in bondage to instant gratification in most areas of life. The machines that only yesterday dazzled you with their lightning speed now infuriate you with their snail-like movement. The hectic pace of your life is like an incessant drumbeat pulsating in your consciousness.

This NOW generation lacks the ancient discipline of patience. The scriptures have been trying to teach us:

"But those who wait for the Lord—who expect, look for and hope in Him—shall change and renew their strength and power; they shall lift their wings and mount up [close to God] as eagles [mount up to the sun]; they shall run and not be weary; they shall walk and not faint or become tired," (Isaiah 40:31 Amp.).

The shells are teaching you patience. They were not formed in a day; their creation took time—lots of time. However, at the perfect moment, the moment when your footprints were embedded in the sand, the shell found you. Or was it the other way around? Nevertheless, your meeting is not coincidental. There is meaning in your keen observation of the sand at your feet.

Your cherished collection of shells will teach you that there are some truths worth remembering. If your stay by the sea is to have any lasting spiritual impact on your life, you must take something of lasting value home with you— not simply souvenirs in the shapes of shells and shell fragments.

What will you have in your possession when the rat race begins again, when there is no longer any sand to sweep out of your vehicle or living quarters, and when there is no sunburn to pamper? Will you take anything worthwhile home with you that will remind you of your time in the midst of God's marvelous creation?

Your shells can be on display throughout your home to help you experience the water's edge all over again. God was there, and He is in your home. His handiwork may not be as obvious in your manufactured world. Yet the shells from your seashore holiday will remind you of a simpler place and a time of quiet meditation. Through their simplicity, they speak of this wonderfully crafted world God created for you. In spite of your insignificant rough edges, in the grand scheme of things He holds you and cherishes you just as you take delight in your shell discoveries. Bring these tiny treasures home with you and keep them near you. Be inspired by them.

God promises to take you home with Him when your time on this fragile planet is over so that He can delight in you for all eternity. He is preparing a heavenly home for you so that you can delight in Him and His presence for all eternity. The limitless scope of the seashore from your vantage point can't help but whet your appetite for things that are eternal.

My Broken Shell

On your quest for the perfect shell in pristine condition, you gaze at myriads of shells that are broken and cracked. You see them flawed and desirable only for the trash heap. Other shells parade their imperfections as the waves wash them farther onto the shore. You can't bring yourself to take the time or make the effort to stop long enough to give them a second glance. Heaven forbid that you would waste your precious time by bending down to pick one up. In the pride of your shell hunting, you decide that only the shells that exhibit true perfection will be good enough to grace the hallowed boundaries of your sacred collection.

It is at the height of your most despicable arrogance that you are reminded of your own brokenness. Like the many broken shells that you ignore on the beach, your life is flawed and frayed beyond any hope of human repair. Again, you remember the gracious and merciful honesty of God. The words of His book resound in your ear:

"...There is none righteous, not even one; there is none who understands, there is none who seeks for God; all have turned aside, together they have become useless; there is none who does good, there is not even one," (Romans 3:10-13).

The indictment rings true; your life is a marred shell, broken beyond anyone's desiring. You ask: Who am I to judge these worn shells? Who am I to cast them aside as worthless? I wasn't willing to save any of those broken and fractured shells from the surf. What does God think of me? How does He react to the broken shell of my life and the brokenness around me?

The Ultimate Broken Shell

God in His infinite mercy and grace looked upon the broken shell of your life, and He did something extraordinary, something truly beyond your ability to fully comprehend. God became a man. God left the glories of heaven to experience the agonies and hardships of earth. John's gospel records the amazing testimony:

"And the Word (Jesus) became flesh and dwelt among us, and we saw His glory, glory as of the only begotten from the Father, full of grace and truth." (John 1:14, [emphasis added])

If your life can be understood as analogous to a broken shell, then God came to earth and became a shell. Imagine that! He was a truly perfect shell willing to be broken for your good. A shell willing to be shattered for your redemption and rescue! Christ allowed Himself to endure all of the pain and heart sorrow that life can bring. He alone is revealed as the One willing to experience your brokenness and pain for your eternal benefit.

"For we do not have a high priest who cannot sympathize with our weaknesses, but One who has been tempted in all things as we are, yet without sin. Therefore let us draw near with confidence to the throne of grace, so that we may receive mercy and find grace to help in time of need," (Hebrews 4:15, 16).

The Lord Jesus Christ, the perfect shell, became broken and marred for your ultimate good—to save you all from your sin. In one of the most poignant passages in all of scripture, Christ is described as the suffering servant.

"He was despised and rejected by men; a man of sorrows, and acquainted with grief; and as one from whom men hide their faces he was despised, and we esteemed him not. Surely he has borne our griefs and carried our sorrows; yet we esteemed him stricken, smitten by God, and afflicted. But he was wounded for our transgressions; he was crushed for our iniquities; upon him was the chastisement that brought us peace, and with his stripes we are healed. All we like sheep have gone astray; we have turned every one to his own way; and the Lord has laid on him the iniquity of us all," (Isaiah 53:3-6, ESV).

A few moments ago, you were unwilling to pause long enough to pick up the broken shell that you considered unworthy of your collection. Ironically, your life and the life of that broken shell are more closely related than the eternal distance between your sinful life and the inapproachable glory of the one true and Holy God.

Yet, God sought you, bridged the gap between you and Him, and came to lift you out of the swirling tide of your own sinfulness. God was willing to stoop down and pick up the broken shards of your shattered life and make you whole again.

"But God demonstrates His own love toward us, in that while we were yet sinners, Christ died for us," (Romans 5:8).

Christ is the incarnation of perfect love. If you want to understand real love, look to Christ.

"God showed how much He loved us by sending His only Son into the world so that we might have eternal life through Him. This is real love. It is not that we loved God, but that He loved us and sent His Son as a sacrifice to take away our sins," (I John 4:9-10 NLT).

God demands all that you have to give in exchange for eternal life. Jesus told the story of a traveler who discovered a treasure of tremendous value, "...*and for joy over it he goes and sells all that he has and buys that field,*" (Matt. 13:44 NKJV). On the heels of that story, Jesus adds greater emphasis by telling another story with the same impact.

"Again, the kingdom of heaven is like a merchant seeking beautiful pearls, who, when he had found one pearl of great price, went and sold all that he had and bought it," (Matt. 13:45,46 NKJV).

The conclusion of these back-to-back stories couldn't be more clear. Jesus Christ is the treasure in the field; He is the pearl of great price. There is nothing in your life that is worth more than having Christ. The soothing symphony of the sea has revealed to you what remains hidden to most—the infinite and eternal value of truly knowing Christ as both Savior and Lord.

There are treasures buried right under your feet. Look around you and be amazed at the myriad of gifts that the sea has to give. You don't have to struggle or fight to find them; the ocean breakers give them willingly. In spite of all the treasures you abscond today, sleep well because when you awake, there will be more, many more. More than you can carry back home with you. So whether you select only a few choice treasures, or haul them by the bucket full, these shimmering shells are only a tiny, infinitesimal sliver of the good things that God has given you and has awaiting you in His Kingdom.

He has given you the greatest treasure of all, His only begotten Son—Jesus! Take hold of Christ.

Selah...

A SHELL PRAYER

Gracious and giving God, thank you for the multitude of treasures that You bring into my life. You have given me so much, things I could have never earned or deserved. The shells that I gather along the shore are such a wonderful reminder of the gracious ways that You give to me without hesitation.

Even as every shell has a story to tell, I'm glad that my life story is unfolding in this place. It's reassuring to know that You have a purpose and a plan for my life and that my life matters greatly in Your eyes.

Forgive me for the many times that I have thought that You were too busy or too unconcerned to care about the smallest parts of my life. Just like the smallest shell fragment, I rejoice in knowing that nothing is too small or insignificant to escape Your concern.

As I wait for the gifts that the wind and the waves will bring at the water's edge, teach me a patience that only You can give. Teach me to wait upon You as You patiently smooth the rough edges of my character and spirit. I trust You to do Your wonderful work in my life.

Thank You, most of all, for the gift of Your grace in my life. I praise You for loving me enough to send Your only Son into this sin-broken world to make eternal life possible for me. For the gift of Your beloved Son, I praise You above the heavens. It's in the glorious name of Jesus Christ my Savior that I confidently pray these things. Amen.

SIXTH DAY JOURNAL

"And then God answered: 'Write this. Write what you see…" (Habakkuk 2:2—*The Message)*

I. A Sight To See: "What is God showing me today?"

II. A Shell to Save: "What Truth(s) is God teaching me today?"

"Our task is to live our personal communion with Christ with such intensity as to make it contagious."
—Paul Tournier

III. A Wave to Watch: What circumstances are affecting my life today?

IV. Footprints to Follow: How is this day going to change the way I live?

"How many people have you made homesick for God?"
—Oswald Chambers

THE SEVENTH DAY:

THE SUNSET

"For from the rising of the sun even to its setting,
My name will be great among the nations..."
Malachi 1:11

~

"The west is broken into bars
Of orange, gold, and gray,
Gone is the sun, come are the stars,
The night infolds the day."
—George MacDonald,
Songs of the Summer Nights

The setting of the sun closes the curtain on the drama of the day.

As the sun silently slides below the western horizon and the shafts of brilliant orange sunlight bid a fond farewell to the day, a time for reflection and rest begins. The day is done. The setting sun marks the end of a day of discovery and delights at the water's edge.

Sunset is an invitation to rest. The setting of the sun is God's way of leading you to quiet worship and communion with Him. God offers you this time to cease striving, let go, and relax. *"Be still, and know that I am God."* (Psalm 46:10 ESV)

Mankind is always in a state of restlessness, and tastes change with each new generation. Yet, the rising and setting of the sun is a daily reminder of the constancy and faithfulness of God. The light of the setting sun casts its glow upon our arrogance and our fickle opinions about the grandeur of God's creation. Nineteenth-century author Oscar Wilde wrote, "Nobody of any real culture, for instance, ever talks nowadays about the beauty of sunset. Sunsets are quite old fashioned…to admire them is a distinct sign of provincialism of temperament. Upon the other hand they go on." In spite of man's ever-changing opinions, "…they go on."

Day by day, evening by evening God reveals His glory and greatness. If only you had fresh eyes to look upon the wonders of His world and His way in your life. Even as the twilight falls upon you, God gives one last grand and glorious display of His omnipotence at the water's edge.

As the prophet Malachi proclaimed, *"For from the rising of the sun even to its setting, My name will be great among the nations,"* (Malachi 1:11).

Poet Wallace Stevens likened the day to the reign of a king. "The day of the sun is like the day of a king. It is a promenade in the morning, a sitting on the throne at noon, a pageant in the evening." His words ring true because all through your visit to the water's edge, God displays His majesty and His magnificence like a king in His royal robes.

The pageantry of the sun's final brilliance satisfies your soul in a way that is serene and deeply satisfying. The day is coming to a conclusion. As night falls, it is a time of sacred rest. William Wordsworth wrote of the beauteous evening, "The holy time is quiet as a nun, breathless with adoration."

Welcome Home

A joyous homecoming happened at the water's edge. It happened on the beach. Jesus chose the place where the water meets the land as the location for restoring one of his followers back into the fold. A bountiful breakfast on the beach was the occasion when Jesus welcomed a wayward Peter back into the loving arms of His embrace.

Peter was a man with a nature like ours: headstrong, prideful, impertinent, and prone to wander into the quicksand of presumptuous sin. Peter had boldly pronounced his undying loyalty to Christ only to be humiliated by his own betrayal and denial of Christ. Perhaps that is the worst of all sins—to deny Christ.

Without the fanfare of a rooster's morning reveille, how many times have you denied Christ in your own life? Your own denials become a cruel betrayal of the One who has created you, the One who came for you, the One who was crucified for you, and the One who is calling you to Himself.

If faith has any meaning in your life, maybe it is the outward manifestation of an inward reality, an everlasting friendship that has been kindled between you and God. Peter had denied Christ on three specific occasions as he sat by a fire in the courtyard of the High Priest. Cloaked in firelight, his every denial grew more emphatic than the one before, culminating with his harshest retort, *"Man, I don't know what you're talking about!"* (Luke 22:60 NIV). The rooster's cry only showcased the depth of his treason. Yes, Peter's trust in Christ had turned into treason. Could the remorse that he felt at that moment have been almost too much to bear? Imagine the depth of his pain. Imagine how heartbroken Christ must have felt at that moment.

Like a beachcomber looking for that special shell, Jesus came looking for Peter. It was not an encounter for retribution or retaliation. Christ came to reconcile Peter to Himself. Jesus came to the beach to meet Peter and forgive him. Jesus built a roaring fire and prepared a delicious breakfast on the beach for the very one who had betrayed and disowned Him in His darkest hours.

By the warmth of a fire kindled in the sand, Jesus welcomed Peter back into His eternal family. Christ drew him back with a series of gentle queries. The Scriptures record the reunion:

"So when they had finished breakfast, Jesus said to Simon Peter, 'Simon, son of John, do you love Me more than these?' He said to Him, 'Yes, Lord; You know that I love You,'" (John 21:15).

Jesus understands the weaknesses of his followers. Even as Peter had denied Christ three times, Jesus gave

Peter three opportunities to reaffirm his love for his Savior. Christ does the same in your life. He lovingly seeks in order to save you.

Matthew 16:26 brings everything into perspective. *"What good will it be for a man if he gains the whole world, yet forfeits his soul? Or what can a man give in exchange for his soul?"* (NIV).

Numbering Our Days

The setting sun is a humbling reminder that your walk in this world is for only a brief season. The fading light of day speaks of the twilight of your own life. Maybe the Psalmist sat at the edge of the sea and marveled at the beauty of the setting sun when he penned these immortal words about the mortality of man.

"Show me, O LORD, my life's end and the number of my days; let me know how fleeting is my life. You have made my days a mere handbreadth; the span of my years is as nothing before you. Each man's life is but a breath. *Selah,*" (Psalm 39:4,5 NIV).

There is infinite mystery couched within your own mortality. You do not know when your days on this earth will end. The Scriptures speak of this mystery, *"...Man does not know his time...,"* (Ecclesiastes 9:12).

The sinking sun is a gentle reminder that the length and breadth of your existence on earth has boundaries even as the edge of the ocean sets a boundary on how far the sea can stretch. The coming of nightfall teaches you to look upon your own life span with an eye on eternity. God has woven a sense of the eternal in your heart. *"He has made everything beautiful in its time. He has also set eternity in the hearts of men...,"* (Eccl. 3:11 NIV).

As the shadows lengthen across the water's edge, your entire life span can best be understood as a single grain of sand. The Psalmist described the length of an average life, *"The length of our days is seventy years—or eighty, if we have the strength..."* (Psalm 90:10a NIV).

What are seventy, eighty, ninety, or even one hundred years in comparison with the eons of eternity to come? Rightly did the Psalmist conclude, *"for they quickly pass, and we fly away,"* (Psalm 90:10b NIV).

Now look out over the great expanse of beach as far as your eye can see and imagine that every single grain of sand equals one hundred years. If you accumulated every grain of sand on every beach on every continent of the world, the incalculable span of time that they represented would reveal only the very first day of eternity.

It is true! God has created you for eternity. In the brilliance of a summer's setting sun, there is no better time to take a realistic look at the material and financial investments that you've made in your life. Jesus told a story that has particular relevance for the sunset time of our life.

"And he told them this parable: 'The ground of a certain rich man produced a good crop. He thought to himself, `What shall I do? I have no place to store my crops.' Then he said, `This is what I'll do. I will tear down my barns and build bigger ones, and there I will store all my grain and my goods. And I'll say to myself, "You have plenty of good things laid up for many years. Take life easy; eat, drink and be merry." 'But God said to him, `You fool! This very night your life will be demanded from you. Then who will get what you have prepared for yourself?' This is how it will be with anyone who stores up things for himself but is not rich toward God," (Luke 12:16-21 NIV).

Even as Christ enjoyed a bountiful breakfast on the beach with Peter, He desires the same with you right now. He is closer to you than you can imagine. Every experience you have enjoyed during this week at the water's edge has been a gift from Almighty God. He has fashioned it all for you. Just as you've heard the sound of the mighty breakers of the sea, you've been hearing God's voice speak to the deepest and best places in your heart and soul. Have you been listening? Have you heard His voice calling out to you?

Two Chairs by the Sea

Artists have used their skills to depict the majestic scenery of the seashore with paint and brush. The often painted picture of two white Adirondack chairs overlooking the sea has been one of my favorites. For me, it is the happy, expectant vision of the future.

With my wife of 25 years by my side, I've envisioned us sitting on those two chairs, looking out on the water, embracing all the sights and sounds of God's glorious creation. From this scenic vantage point as husband and wife, we will look back on our decades together, our children, and their children to follow. We'll celebrate God's goodness together as a picturesque incarnation of what the Psalmist wrote, *"Glorify the LORD with me; let us exalt his name together,"* (Psalm 34:3 NIV).

In my limited vision, I now realize that these two chairs by the sea have a spiritual dimension that I had never thought about before. The two chairs represent the life of a person and his or her personal relationship with Jesus Christ. One chair is just for you. God has placed you here by the sea to enjoy it. The other chair is for the Lord Jesus Christ. He loves the beach as much as you do. Even more, He loves you with a love than cannot be fathomed by the human mind. He loves you more than the stars of the sky. He loves you more than all the grains of sand on all the shores that encircle this incredible world. God says, *"I have loved you with an everlasting love...,"* (Jeremiah 31:3).

Christ has invited you to this place by the sea. He has prepared it especially for your enjoyment and spiritual edification. Hear His invitation. Know that He wants to sit with you by the sea both now and for all eternity. He longs for you to invite Him into the center of your life. You'll enjoy a spiritual meal, a breakfast on the beach, like you've never known before. Jesus is saying to you, *"Listen! I stand at the door and knock. If anyone hears My voice and opens the door, I will come in to him and have dinner with him, and he with Me,"* (Revelation 3:20 HCSB).

In this sacred place by the sea, open your spiritual eyes and look into the great expanse of the sea. Christ's love for you is deeper than the ocean's depths. Listen to the soothing sound of the waves. They echo the risen Savior's voice. *"...His voice was like the sound of many waters,"* (Rev. 1:15). Even though you can't see Him, Christ is right here with you. Does this seem too good to be true? It is true! This truth can change the course of your life on this earth, and it can change the direction of your destiny into the splendors of eternity.

Say "Yes!" to Him

As Christ sat by the sea, He asked Peter the most important question that anyone will ever hear. It's the very same question that Christ is asking you right now. Jesus is asking, "Do you love me? Do you really love me?"

How will you answer? Can you say with honesty and conviction, "Yes, Lord, You know that I love You."

You are here by the sea reading these words for only one reason: you are loved by God. He wants to make sure that you know it. He smiled the day you were born. He knows you better than you know yourself. He looks right at you and He says, "Yes! You're the one I want!"

Sound unbelievable? Every person who has ever lived has turned his or her back on God's love. God calls our rejection "sin." Sin is not a very trendy word, and it's not a very pretty picture. Sin describes the fact that all of mankind has failed the test and willfully wandered way off course. There's one word that describes our spiritual situation: "guilty."

Now there is one simple word that describes God. It's the word "Holy." The word means 100 percent good and 100 percent pure in character, thought, and action. This presents a real problem; our sin has separated us from the one true God. Yet deep within the heart of mankind, there is a passion to be connected to God.

Like two close friends sitting in Adirondack chairs looking out into the beauty of the sea, Christ wants to share a personal and eternal friendship with you. You can't see Jesus with your physical eyes, but you can trust Him and get to know Him better. You don't see Him now, but He's alive and He's present in your life. You can have a friendship with Him that is more intimate and satisfying than any other you'll ever experience.

Jesus Christ is on bended knee. He is waiting for you to say "Yes" to Him just as Peter did. You don't have to do anything to initiate this friendship with Jesus because He has already initiated it. How? Jesus suffered and died on the cross in your place. He took the punishment for your sin. He scrubbed away your guilt, and He remembers your sin no more. If you will accept what He has already done for you by faith, then there will be no obstruction between you and God.

If you've marveled at His good creation and heard His voice in the waves and the wind, you will know that He's alive, too. You are reading these words for just a brief time in your life, but God will continue to speak to your heart long after you have laid down this book and left the water's edge.

God will continue to speak to you because He wants you to know how much He loves you. Every time you hear the ocean's roar, or watch a seagull circle overhead, or pick up a shell from the sea, you'll know that God is not going to give up on you. His invitation is clear.

How you can begin to love God back? Just talk to him, friend to friend, the way Peter did. Prayer is the way we talk to Him. You can talk to God using these words or you can close this book and speak to God with the words of your own choosing. The important thing is that you start the conversation *now*.

"Dear Jesus, thank You for loving me. I believe that You are God's only begotten Son, the eternal God-Man. I believe that You died on the cross in my place to make a way for me to know You and love You forever. I know that I have sinned and need forgiveness. Forgive me, Jesus, and take away the stains that sin has left in my life. Yes, Lord, I love you with all my heart. I believe that You are alive, and I trust You to change me. Teach me to hear Your voice and follow Your way. I pray this in Jesus' name. Amen."

The Rest of the Story

For those who have begun a forever friendship with Christ, the sermon of the sunset is no longer discouraging. The sunset graciously reminds you that your days upon this earth will eventually come to an end. The end of your days is not the end of the story, however. The setting of the sun is just a foreshadow of the glorious things that await God's children. Rightly did Clement of Alexandria say, "Christ has turned all our sunsets into dawns."

Because we know and love Christ, the specter of physical death is no longer the haunting fear that it once was. Billy Graham said, "Someday you will read or hear that Billy Graham is dead. Don't you believe a word of it! I shall be more alive then than I am now. I will just have changed my address. I will have gone into the presence of God."

The Beginning of the Great Story

The sunset is a glorious curtain closing and marking the end of a single day. As the sun dips beneath the western horizon, you see a glimpse of the brevity of your own earthly life. Your time on this tiny planet is momentary, but your days spent under the circle of the sun are not the end. Your days of eternity are just beginning.

Your present life is but a prelude to the limitless reaches of eternity. C.S. Lewis' classic children's tale, *The Chronicles of Narnia,* concludes with a poignant and poetic glimpse of what lies ahead after your days on earth are over. "The term is over: the holidays have begun. The dream is ended: this is the morning."

There is a great temptation to live, work, and dream as if your present life is the culmination and the sum total of what it means to be alive. With your vision focused on the sandcastles of your own making, you often miss the glorious sunset, which is a foretaste of the splendors that await.

Lewis' enduring allegory whets our appetite for eternity with these thrilling words.

"And for us this is the end of all the stories, and we can most truly say that they all lived happily ever after. But for them it was only the beginning of the real story. All their life in this world and all their adventures in Narnia had only been the cover and the title page: now at last they were beginning Chapter One of the Great Story, which no one on earth has read: which goes on for ever: in which every chapter is better than the one before."[2]

As the sun sets in your life, whether it is for a season, a time at the water's edge, or the end of your time on earth, in Him you have nothing to fear as the darkness invades your world. The ancient Israelites were given a pillar of cloud by day as a reminder of the Lord's nearness and protection. At night, there was the brilliant and awe-inspiring pillar of fire to remind them of the Lord's watchful care even in the darkness. You have nothing to fear in the setting of the sun. The darkness cannot overtake you if you are a child of the day.

It is reassuring to know that as you face the darkness in your life, you need not fear the dark. God goes before you into the twilight and into the blackness of night. The Psalmist rejoiced to know, *"For You light my lamp; The Lord my God illumines my darkness,"* (Psalm 18:28).

As the sun sets, the Lord provides you with a faith and a confidence in Him that pierces the deepest darkness. He illumines your darkest midnight. As the light fades and the darkness descends, hear His gentle whisper, "Fear Not."

Selah...

A Sunset Prayer

Lord of creation, thank You for the day that has now come to its end. I rejoice in the events and activities of this day—the joys and happiness that have thrilled my heart. I thank You for the challenges that this day has brought. May the difficulties of this day help me to depend on You more totally and completely than I did when this day began.

As the sun slips beneath the horizon of the earth, I pray that I've learned to love You just a little bit more. I pray that the experiences of this day have given me a better understanding of just how exalted and magnificent You truly are.

As this day ends and my thoughts turn toward the day to come, give me a restful night. If You choose to bring another day into existence, help me to begin it with my heart and mind focused on You and Your glory.

Teach me to number my days and to live each day in such a way that You will be honored and glorified by the actions I take and the attitudes that I embrace. Give me spiritual eyes to see that my days on this earth are just a prelude to the joys and purposes that You have for me in Your presence for all eternity.

I pray this in the name of the one who is the Alpha and Omega, the beginning and the end, Jesus Christ the Lord. Amen.

SEVENTH DAY JOURNAL

"And then God answered: 'Write this. Write what you see..." (Habakkuk 2:2—*The Message*)

I. A Sight To See: What is God showing me today?

II. A Shell to Save: What truth(s) is God teaching me today?

"Life is a voyage that's homeward bound."
—Herman Melville

III. A Wave to Watch: What circumstances are affecting my life today?

IV. Footprints to Follow: How is this day going to change the way I live?

"Life is a glorious opportunity, if it is used to condition us for eternity. If we fail in this, though we succeed in everything else, our life will have been a failure.."
—Billy Graham

THE BEACH AT MY BACK

"But you will not leave in haste or go in flight; for the Lord will go before you and the God of Israel will be your rear guard."

Isaiah 52:12 (NIV)

~

"It is easy to turn our religious life into a cathedral for beautiful memories, but there are feet to be washed, hard flints to be walked over, people to be fed. Very few of us go there, but that is the way the Son of God went."

— Oswald Chambers

When you find God at the water's edge, your life will never be the same.

You are not leaving the beach. Instead, you are embarking upon the greatest adventure of your life as you seek a closer relationship to God. The water's edge has been a place of refuge and respite. Your spirit has been refreshed and your soul has been replenished by the very presence of God.

Your time by the sea has given you an unhurried, uncluttered chance to enjoy your relationship with God. Even now, God will use your memories of the seashore to shape your perspective. You will view the water's edge through changed eyes. More importantly, you will look at your own life through eyes focused on forever.

You have been given a sacred gift, a new lens, a better camera, a clearer vision, and new insight into your life. You've experienced an enjoyable companionship with the Creator at the water's edge.

Traveling Lighter

Your bags are bulging with belongings, and your suitcases are overflowing with the souvenirs that will remind you of this blessed season by the sea. The premises appear unnaturally devoid of the objects and the people that have made this your home for these hours and days at the water's edge. This time and place has provided you with an unfamiliar clarity and given you a bird's eye view of God's glorious creation.

You have been given an opportunity to jettison the excess baggage of your cluttered and crowded life on the mainland. This trip to the shore has reminded you of the joys of a simpler life and has renewed your dream of traveling with a lighter load through the days that lie ahead.

Traveling lighter won't be easy; and, yet, there are attitudes, perceptions, and preconceived notions that would be best left behind. Let them go in order to live the kind of God-filled life that you are longing to live. You enjoyed this sacred time with the Savior, and you learned that His call to you will mean letting go of some material things and frivolous activities that have been weighing you down. You hear the promise that only Christ can offer.

"Come to Me, all you who are weary and burdened, and I will give you rest. Take My yoke upon you and learn from Me, for I am gentle and humble in heart, and you will find rest for your souls. For My yoke is easy and My burden is light," (Matthew 11:28-30 NIV).

Now is not the time for timid living. The shelter where you've spent your days by the sea has not been shaken by hurricane winds. The contemplative time, the joy-soaked gourmet life that you've enjoyed at the edge of the sea may have shaken your former priorities into a new order. Well-won memories now hang from the walls like framed paintings in a nicely-appointed household.

With the beach at your back, you make the radical transition from a time of wonder and introspection to the work of the clock-ruled world. Perhaps you feel like a deep-sea diver who has been swimming in the depths of the sea only to rise to the surface again. You must rise cautiously and slowly through the waters of these blessed days by the sea to avoid the catastrophic sickness that can occur when a diver rises too quickly from the depths of the sea to the surface.

The pressures have changed dramatically in your life in the past few days. Your season by the sea has been a depressurizing time. The pressures of the workaday world have been washed away in the surf. The release of tensions has been both intoxicating and liberating.

You have known the serenity of the sea and delighted yourself in the soft, seductive sound of the waves that has soothed your soul. Even in the midst of your busyness at the beach, there has been a rejuvenating absence of pressure, stress, and the nerve-racking demands that are your constant companions back in the "real" world of work, school, and chores.

As you turn your back on the beach and come to grips with the fact that you must leave the water's edge, you begin to feel the pressures of your life returning. One of the not-so-slight side effects of this transition is a returning sense of responsibility with its attendant feeling of life pressure.

A sense of melancholy begins to set in. Call it post-vacation syndrome. There is a foreboding sense of pensive reflection that rules your emotions at the thought of leaving this place of tranquility. It is only natural to recoil from the gravity of the tidal wave pulling you back into the world of housework, bills, yard work, homework, and the ebb and flow of the office, work, paperwork, meetings, and the life politics that must be faced once again.

Leaving the Mountaintop

Turn your back to the beach and consider how Jesus' three closest compatriots must have felt. Peter, James, and John had been in a holy place at a holy moment. With their own eyes, they had feasted upon the indescribable splendor of the transfigured Christ. This miraculous experience on the mountaintop is recorded in chapter seventeen of Matthew's gospel.

For a few fleeting moments, God pulled back the curtain on eternity and allowed the outshining radiance of Christ in all His resplendent glory to flood our world. This inner circle of three was overwhelmed and exhilarated by the brilliance and splendor of the transfigured Christ. True to the spirit of many of Jesus' followers, both then and now, when in doubt as to what to do next, start a building program! "Don't just stand there, build something, anything!" has been the rallying cry of Christ followers for the better part of two millennia now.

Peter started the trend when he said, *"Lord, it is good for us to be here; if You wish, I will make three tabernacles here, one for You, and one for Moses, and one for Elijah,"* (Matthew 17:4).

There was revelation and revival on the mountaintop, so why shouldn't Peter have wanted to stay. For these disciples, the mountaintop has been their cathedral, a glorious place of life-altering worship. Following Christ's footsteps along the shore has brought you to the same sort of cathedral.

You have walked with the Savior as He has left His footprints in the sand. You have walked with Him in a spirit of worship and adoration. The Lord's presence has refreshed you like the waves that have splashed across your feet.

Your natural desire is to remain at the shore to inhale the splendiferous sensations that can only be embraced by the sea. The wish expressed by artist Doris Morgan has found a place in our own hearts. "If my dreams could all come true, Paradise would be—in a little bungalow—somewhere...by the sea."

How else can the building boon by the sea be explained? Fifty percent of the world's population, three billion people, lives within sixty kilometers of the beach. Our love affair with the beach is stronger than ever. Half of the U.S. population, 150 million people, live within fifty miles of the coast. All across the globe, what were once desolate, uninhabited strips of beach accessible only by four-wheel vehicles a few years ago are now lined with million-dollar mansions, hotels, resorts, and condos stacked like cordwood along these precious slivers of shoreline.

Since you have basked in the satisfying sensations of the seashore, your desire is to linger there rather than leave. Yet, it is time to return to the stuff of inland life. A place by the sea is a soothing site for a season of respite and reflection. The water's edge is a seductive temptress, and you must resist her siren song to stay beyond your time.

As the disciples descended from the peak, so the beachcomber musters the resolve to shake the sand from his sandals and begin the journey inland. Turn your backs to the beach for the same reasons Peter, James, and John left the mountaintop. The disciples descended from lofty heights to face the fury of Satan's cruel mockery and torment. A man distraught over the mental, emotional, and physical state of his son was desperately seeking help from Jesus' disciples. *"I brought him to Your disciples, and they could not cure him,"* (Matthew 17:16). Jesus rebuked the demon that had taken control of the young boy's life, and then He taught His disciples a critically important lesson.

"Why could we not drive it out?" was their perplexing query. Jesus' answer is sobering: *"Because of the littleness of your faith…,"* (Matthew 17:20a).

What the disciples had seen and experienced in the glorious radiance of the mountaintop of Transfiguration had not translated to a greater level of confidence and absolute dependence upon Christ. They had just witnessed Christ exalted over Moses, the lawgiver; and Elijah, the mightiest prophet; and yet, their faith had not grown any stronger.

Your sisal sack is filled, your bags are packed, your memories and souvenirs have been collected, stored, and are now loaded for the return trip into the realm of the real world with all its rigors and responsibilities. Fear not. The communion that you have experienced is a prelude. It is not the end. It is only the beginning— a *better* beginning because God does not want you to stay in a place where faith and trust cannot grow. Faith grows as you return to face the good fight. God wants you where the fires are burning; that's where you need to be.

The disciples enjoyed the fellowship at the peak of the mountain, but there was a man racked with desperation and concern for his son. The disciples needed to be in the valley, not on the mountain peak. It is in the valleys of life where you find your calling and your purpose. Where life intersects with hurt and sorrow and questions is where God is leading you.

Oswald Chambers said it well. "It is easy to turn our religious life into a cathedral for beautiful memories, but there are feet to be washed, hard flints to be walked over, people to be fed. Very few of us go there, but that is the way the Son of God went."[3]

Follow Me

Jesus encountered a broken-hearted, guilt-ridden Peter and lovingly drew him back into the fold of the faith. Christ prepared a beautiful breakfast on the beach for His disciples, and He has prepared a magnificent meal for you as well. Christ changes everything! Look what He did in Peter's life.

In the gloom of night, Peter had denied Christ three times by the light of a fire that had been kindled by those who hated Jesus.

As the rising sun welcomed a new day, Jesus kindled a blazing fire on the beach and gave Peter three opportunities to reaffirm his love for the Lord. Now the Lord has done this in your life as well. He has lovingly kindled a fire in your soul by the edge of the sea. With the flames of His purpose burning bright in your heart, you can leave this place with a bold new outlook on life.

Jesus called Peter and then He commissioned Peter with two simple words. When Peter had declared his love for Christ the third time, the Lord revealed the future of Peter's life and death and said, *"Follow Me!"* (John 21:19).

Your future, from this day forward and forever, can be summarized by these same two simple words. Jesus is speaking to your heart, "Follow Me!"

Your time at the place where the water meets the land has been a place where God has refreshed and restored you to a proper understanding of His working in your life and in the wider world. What you've experienced here on the shore is what the Lord of heaven and earth wants you to live out in the dirty, messy realities of the days that stretch before you.

If you truly desire to follow Christ from this moment on, it will cost you something. The cost of following Christ is high. It will cost you everything. It will cost you your life. Jesus said it himself. *"... 'If anyone desires to come after Me, let him deny himself, and take up his cross daily, and follow Me,"* (Luke 9:23 NKJV).

All of the twelve disciples, except one, were martyred for their willingness to follow Christ all the way to a sure and certain, violent death. This intrepid band of Jesus followers clearly understood what Pastor John MacArthur has called "the high cost and the infinite value of following Christ." They literally turned the world upside down. Nothing in the world has been the same since Christ's disciples lived and died for the greater glory of God.

Down through the centuries, the light of the gospel has been faithfully passed from one generation of followers to the next. Now the light has come into your heart and life. It is time for you to follow Christ no matter where He leads, no matter what the price. Jesus said, *"For whoever wants to save his life will lose it, but whoever loses his life for me will find it,"* (Matt. 16:25 NIV).

As you turn your back to the beach, you have Christ's assurance that wherever you go the Lord is with you anywhere and everywhere the sole of your foot touches the earth. The Lord is your constant companion, not limited by the constraints of geography or locale.

The Psalmist proclaimed,

"Where can I go from Your Spirit? Or where can I flee from Your presence? If I ascend to heaven, You are there; If I make my bed in Sheol, behold, You are there. If I take the wings of the dawn, If I dwell in the remotest part of the sea, even there Your hand will lead me, and Your right hand will lay hold of me," (Psalm 139: 7-10).

Selah…

A Leaving Prayer
(A Prayer with My Back to the Beach)

Gracious and Giving God, I rejoice in the past days that You have so graciously and generously allowed me to enjoy. You have filled each day with happiness and experiences that only You could bring. The sound of the surf, the vastness of the sky, the softness of the sand, and the immensity of the sea have all wonderfully reflected a glimmer of Your limitless glory.

As I turn to leave the water's edge, make me mindful of the testimony of Your creation. You have been a constant comfort and the source of my serenity that I've experienced in this splendid place.

Teach me to remember the lessons that You have taught me by the sea. Help me to wage war against forgetfulness. Bring to my mind those things that are in keeping with Your revealed will and Your purpose for my life.

If You should choose, prepare a place and a time when You can bring me back to this sacred part of Your creation. Thank You, Lord, for this time we've enjoyed together at the edge of Your Ocean.

I pray these things in the strong and mighty name of Jesus, my Savior and Lord. Amen.

THE BEACH AT MY BACK JOURNAL

"And then God answered: 'Write this. Write what you see..." (Habakkuk 2:2—*The Message*)

I. A Sight To See: What has God shown me this week?

II. A Shell to Save: What truth(s) has God taught me this week?

"To have found God is not an end in itself but a beginning."
—Franz Rosenzweig

III. A Wave to Watch: What circumstances will affect my life in the future?

IV. Footprints to Follow: How is this week going to change the way I live?

"I thank thee, O Lord, that thou hast so set eternity within my heart that no earthly thing can ever satisfy me wholly."
—John Baillie

—Notes—

1. Edythe Draper, *Draper's Book of Quotations for the Christian World* © 1992 (Wheaton, Illinois: Tyndale House Publishers, Inc.), #4748, p. 256.

2. C.S. Lewis, *The Last Battle* (New York: Macmillan Publishing Company, First Collier Books Edition, 1970, p. 184.

3. Edythe Draper, *Draper's Book of Quotations for the Christian World* © 1992 (Wheaton, Illinois: Tyndale House Publishers, Inc.), #4748, p. 559.

ABOUT THE AUTHOR

Mark Jordan graduated with a B.S. in Communications from the University of Tennessee at Knoxville in 1980. He earned the Master of Divinity and Doctor of Ministry degrees from the Southwestern Baptist Theological Seminary in Fort Worth, Texas.

Since 1987, Mark has served as the senior pastor of the Ironbridge Baptist Church—a young, vibrant congregation in the suburbs of Richmond, Virginia. He has written articles for a variety of Christian publications including *Focus on the Family*, *Home Life*, and *Living with Teenagers*.

Mark and his wife Pal live in Chester, Virginia. They have three children.

—To Order—

Breakfast at the Beach:
Finding God at the Water's Edge
by Mark R. Jordan

If unavailable at your favorite bookstore,
Order from Mark Jordan at
www.breakfastonthebeach.com

or
—Call 1-800-864-1648—
Postal Orders: Send to
LangMarc Publishing
P.O. Box 90488
Austin, Texas 78709-0488
email: langmarc@booksails.com

Breakfast on the Beach: USA $12.95 + $2.50 postage
Canada: $16.95 (TX. residents add tax 8.25%)

Send _____ copies of *Breakfast on the Beach* to

Name: _____

Street Address: _____

City, State _____

Phone Number: _____

Check enclosed for $ _____

Credit Card: _____

Expiration: _____

Printed in the United States
124048LV00002B/130-156/A